D0362319

"The authors of this wonderful boo[k]
cality to cut through the many com[plexities]
and families in today's troubled times. They show precisely
how ordinary people can help change the world of individual
children, of whole communities, and—ultimately—of the
nation."

    —Lisbeth B. Schorr, Harvard University, author of *Within Our Reach: Breaking the Cycle of Disadvantage*

"*Every Kid Counts* is a powerful collaborative work that presents thirty-one concrete and important ways that parents and concerned adults can make a positive and substantial difference in the lives of our children. This book by Margaret Brodkin and Coleman Advocates provides parents with a 'checklist' of issues that are key to our children's development. We can make a difference, and this book shows us how. It is both practical and inspirational. Every parent should read *Every Kid Counts*."

    —James Comer, M.D., Maurice Falk Professor of Child Psychiatry, Yale Child Study Center, author of *Maggie's American Dream*

"A resource that underscores the urgency of children's needs at a time when America is poised to do more for the healthy development of all children."

    —Alvin F. Poussaint, M.D., Harvard University, coauthor of *Raising Black Children* and consultant to *The Bill Cosby Show*

EVERY KID COUNTS

EVERY KID COUNTS

COUNTS

31 WAYS
TO SAVE
OUR CHILDREN

Margaret Brodkin
and
Coleman Advocates for Children & Youth

Illustrated by Gwen Gordon

HarperSanFrancisco
A Division of HarperCollins*Publishers*

FIRST EDITION

Library of Congress Cataloging-in-Publication Data

Brodkin, Margaret.
    Every kid counts: 31 ways to save our children / Margaret Brodkin & Coleman Advocates for Children & Youth.
        p.   cm.
    Includes bibliographical references.
    ISBN 0-06-250213-1
    1. Child welfare—United States.   2. Children—United States—social conditions.   I. Coleman Advocates for Children & Youth.
    II. Title.
    HV741.B8   1993
    362.7'1'0973—dc20   91–56412
                                                                              CIP

93   94   95   96   97   ❖   CWI   10   9   8   7   6   5   4   3   2   1

This edition is printed on acid-free paper that meets the American National Standards Institute Z39.48 Standard.

To PIONEER CHILDREN'S ADVOCATE Jean Jacobs. Her belief that the protection of our children requires the compassion and common sense of all of us is the theme of this book.

Thirty years ago, Jean Jacobs found a neighbor's lost baby being held behind bars in San Francisco's county juvenile hall. Her outrage led to a lifelong battle to improve conditions for children. She began at home, by contacting interested friends. Working out of her living room, this small group became Citizens for Juvenile Justice. Ultimately, the group pressured the city to cut by half the number of children locked up in the ineffective and inhumane detention center.

Jean's outrage about the plight of children and the unjust treatment they often receive from the bureaucracies intended to help them led to the creation of Coleman Advocates for Children & Youth. Jean, still an active member of the board of directors, continues to inspire our work. Her message that making life better for children is too important to be left to "agencies" and "officials" has had a profound effect. Jean Jacobs demonstrates what a single committed and persistent individual of unrelenting integrity and purpose can accomplish for her community's children.

Contents

Part 1.
31 Ways to Save Our Children

Part 2.
Reviewing the Basics:
Skills You Need to Make Every Kid Count

Acknowledgments

THIS BOOK REFLECTS THE WORK of many knowledgeable, committed people—a truly remarkable network of child advocates. The authors for the following chapters were:

1. *Turn Off the Tube:* Terry Strauss, independent film producer.
2. *Champion Public Education:* Judith Christensen, high school teacher, San Francisco Unified School District. 3. *Have Fun with a Kid:* Carol Hotnit-Callen, Assistant Director, Coleman Advocates for Children & Youth. 7. *Help a Child Avoid Having a Child:* Claire D. Brindis, Director of Center for Reproductive and Health Policy Research, Institute for Health Policy Studies, University of California, San Francisco. 9. *Include Children with Disabilities:* Juno Duenas, Executive Director, Support for Parents with Special Children. 10. *Keep a Child's Creative Spirit Alive:* Dana Smith, Fund Raiser/Publicist, Coleman Advocates for Children & Youth. 11. *Feed a Hungry Child:* Laurie True, Senior Policy Analyst, California Food Policy Advocates. 12. *Hire a Youth:* Kristen Bachler, Executive Director, San Francisco Delinquency Prevention Commission. 13. *Make Your Company Child-Friendly:* Blaine Townsend, free-lance writer. 14. *Unlearn Prejudice: They're All Our Children:* Gwen Gordon, illustrator and writer, Kristen Bachler, Executive Director, San Francisco Delinquency Prevention Commission, and Lorraine Honig, Board of Directors, Coleman Advocates for Children & Youth. 15. *Stop Cigarette Ads from Killing Our Kids:* Stanton A. Glantz, Ph.D., Professor of Medicine, University of California, San Francisco. 16. *Just Say No to the Liquor Lobby:* Andrew McGuire, Executive Director, Trauma Foundation, University of California, San Francisco. 18. *Make Children's Health Care a Right:* Dana Hughes, Senior Policy Analyst, Institute for

Health Policy Studies, University of California, San Francisco. *21. Make Your Neighborhood Safe for Kids:* Carol Hotnit-Callen, Assistant Director, Coleman Advocates for Children & Youth. *23. Fight for Car Seats, Helmets, and Smoke Detectors:* Andrew McGuire, Executive Director, Trauma Foundation, University of California, San Francisco. *24. Face the Fact That Children Get AIDS:* Janet Shalwitz, M.D., Director of Special Programs for Youth, San Francisco Department of Public Health. *26. Befriend a Homeless Family:* Jeanie Kortum-Stermer, Program Director, Hamilton Family Shelter, and Board of Directors, Coleman Advocates for Children & Youth. *29. Empower Kids to Save the Earth:* Dana Smith, Fund Raiser/Publicist, Coleman Advocates for Children & Youth. *Give Resources: How to Be an Effective Donor:* Dana Smith, Fund Raiser/Publicist, Coleman Advocates for Children & Youth.

The following people provided extremely useful early drafts, creative ideas, and background research: Gary Beringer, Executive Director, San Francisco Educational Services, on education; Martha Roditti, faculty, San Francisco State University, Dept. of Social Work Education, on child care; Kristen Bebelar, therapist, and Kathy Baxter, Executive Director, San Francisco Child Abuse Council, on family violence and child abuse; Irma Dillard, Program Director, Youth Advocates, on runaway youth and prejudice; Michelle Magee, Associate Director, Youth Advocates, on runaway youth; Jeffrey Callen, President, Legal Write, on neighborhood safety; Dan MacAllair, Project Director, Center on Juvenile and Criminal Justice, on juvenile justice; Wayne Clark, Ph.D., Director of Community Substance Abuse Services, San Francisco Department of Public Health, on drug abuse; Eva Maas, Coleman Advocates for Children & Youth, on parenting. Dana Smith, Coleman Advocates for Children & Youth, offered countless creative suggestions and insights on every subject covered in the book.

Merle Bachman expertly edited and patiently made sense of the unwieldy early draft, and contributed significantly and with great insight to many chapters, including the chapters on disabilities, volunteering, immigrant children, and intergenerational programming. Dan Bellum skillfully edited four key chapters. Angel Brunner, Sara M. Lake, and Carol Hotnit-Callen provided important background research on many topics; Wendy Peverill-Conti provided essential organizational oversight. Jeff Huggins from Foote, Cone, and Belding offered helpful editing suggestions.

Fortunately for all concerned, Gwen Gordon happened into Coleman's office one day as we were discussing the book. Recruiting her as the illustrator was just plain good luck.

This book would not have been possible without the involvement and encouragement of the Coleman Advocates for Children & Youth Board of Directors.

The enthusiasm of the staff at HarperSanFrancisco contributed greatly to the book. Naomi Lucks brought more than great copy editing skills to the project. Her commitment to the message of the book assured that the book was truly user-friendly.

This book would not have been written were it not for senior editor John Loudon, who approached Coleman with the concept of the book, and whose vision guided the project.

Thanks to all of these individuals, and to many others too numerous to list, who reviewed chapters and made suggestions. We are grateful to all the child advocates whose individual and group actions inspired this book.

Margaret Brodkin
Executive Director,
Coleman Advocates for Children & Youth

Preface:
A True Children's Story

**How a Small Group of Ordinary Citizens
Challenged the Political "Powers that Be"
and—Against All Odds—Won $170 Million Dollars
for Children's Services**

ONCE UPON A TIME, the boys and girls of San Francisco were happy. They had toys to play with, and plenty of food to eat. But over the years, their lives grew bleak and they became sad. Their schools began to fall apart. They had no safe places to play. And many got sick because their mommies and daddies didn't have enough money for doctors.

"Who will help us?" asked the boys and girls.

"*We can't*," said the politicians. "Boys and girls don't vote or donate money to our campaigns."

"*We can't*," said the business community. "It costs too much money. It will interfere with our profits."

"*We can't*," said the bureaucrats. "We have to follow too many rules and regulations."

Finally, in desperation, the boys and girls asked a little nonprofit children's organization. "We're not very big," said the 21 board members and four staff members of the little organization. But when they saw the tears in the children's eyes, they got an idea. "What if the city charter *guaranteed* that children get their fair share of funding each year in the city budget? Then there would be money for playgrounds, libraries, and health care. Then children wouldn't have to compete with grown-up special interests.

"We will put our idea on the ballot, so that all San Franciscans can vote on whether children should get special priority. We will call it the Children's Amendment," said the little children's organization.

But many people were skeptical. *"You can't do that,"* they said.

"The amendment will tie our hands," said every elected official.

"San Francisco is an adult city. You will have too many powerful opponents," said the superstar political consultant.

"Ballot-box budgeting is bad public policy," said the learned professors of the leading universities.

"This is special-interest politics," said the Chamber of Commerce.

"We think we can," said the little children's organization. "We believe that the ordinary citizens of San Francisco want to help the boys and girls. They will know best. Yes indeed, we think we can. We think we can. *We think we can.*"

And they began to work.

- They gathered 68,000 signatures on petitions to put the Children's Amendment on the ballot—more signatures than had been gathered for any other petition in the city's history.

"I think I can. I think I can. I think I can,"
said the Little Children's Organization.

- They put signs up all over the city that said, "SF ♥ Kids."
- They talked to over 100 neighborhood groups about the plight of the city's children.
- They went on talk shows, distributed fact sheets, made a video, and enlisted the help of hundreds of parents, youth, and other committed community members.

One day children took over City Hall. Pulling little red wagons stacked with petitions, they submitted the 68,000 signatures to the Registrar of Voters, as the adult "power brokers" looked on.

The *New York Times* took note, reporting that San Franciscans were bypassing the traditional political establishment and taking the problems of children into their own hands. Pretty soon all of San Francisco was talking about how much they cared about children.

After a while almost all the politicians supported the Children's Amendment. Most of them wore a little button that said, "I ♥ kids."

The arguments against the Children's Amendment began to fall apart. Many people began to understand what the little children's organization had been saying: that "ballot-box budgeting" was the essence of democracy, that investing in children was a cost-savings, not an expense, and that caring about children was the antidote for "special interest" politics.

Opponents of the measure began to avoid the press. They refused to debate the representatives of the little children's organization.

Then ABC News and CBS News declared the Children's Amendment a groundbreaking policy initiative for the whole country to watch.

On November 5, 1991, San Francisco became the first city in the country to guarantee funding for children each year in its city budget. And on election night it was the voters of San Francisco—not the politicians, pundits, or experts—who celebrated the triumph of their *own* good judgment and concern for their city's children. "We knew we could. We knew we could. We knew we would," smiled the little children's organization. And all the children of San Francisco smiled too.

Coleman Advocates for Children & Youth is the "little children's organization" in this true story. We were just 25 people—a lawyer, a day-care teacher, a nun, a police officer, a computer consultant, a writer, a school principal, an ex-Peace Corps volunteer, several homemakers, some students, and a few social workers. We thought we were too small to make a difference, but during that election we learned the lesson of a lifetime.

We learned that ordinary people can take matters into their own hands when it comes to the welfare of our children. We learned that together we had the skills and power to turn a city around. We learned that it is only when the will of the people is ignored that a community can neglect its children.

WE NOW KNOW FOR CERTAIN that it is people like us—people like you—who are going to save America's children.

Why You Need to Care

These are all our children. We will all profit by, or pay for, whatever they become.

—James Baldwin

WHAT IS HAPPENING to our children?

The quality of childhood is deteriorating, and every caring American knows something is wrong:

- Our kids aren't learning the skills they need to survive in a demanding future.

- Many parents spend so much time scrambling between jobs and child care that they have almost no time to talk to children about what they want for lunch, much less explore what they think and feel.

- Most kids spend three hours or more a day sitting passively in front of the TV instead of playing creatively—and what's worse, it isn't even safe for our youngest children to play in the neighborhood park.

- When childhood ends, young adults of all races and all economic classes find they must continue living with their parents because they can't afford to live on their own. For the first time in our nation's history, children are economically worse off than their parents.

It is impossible to ignore the utter despair of our most disadvantaged children:

- One in four children under age six lives in poverty. Half of the people who become poor each year in America are now children.

- Entire families are living on America's streets, homeless and begging for food.

- A growing number of our babies are born underweight and unhealthy—higher than the percentage in 30 other countries.

- 30% of the kids who enter ninth grade do not graduate from high school four years later—many have given up before their life really even starts.

- Teen suicides have tripled in the past 30 years.

What is happening to our values? We place a higher value on tax benefits for the wealthy, the profits of the liquor industry, and the political influence of the gun lobby than on the well-being of our children. We should hardly be surprised about (or blame the values of our families for) the fact that our teen pregnancy rate is the highest in the industrialized world, that half of our youngsters drink, and that one in twenty kids carries firearms to school at least once a month.

Even if our own children are not among the worst off, they will suffer. Our country will be spending so much money controlling its disenfranchised people that it will not have the resources to provide a decent quality of life for the rest. This is already happening—prison budgets are climbing, while education budgets are plummeting. Right now, the United States locks up a greater percentage of its children than any country in the developed world.

Every Kid Counts!

We simply cannot afford to let any child's potential be wasted.

Our children are an increasingly diverse population. In some states, such as California, the majority of children are already children of color. Experts now estimate that this will be true nationwide by the middle of the next century. We must stop thinking of our least-advantaged children as "other people's children."

We used to think we could rely on every child's family to take care of its own problems. But the traditional family that we associate with the 1950s—a two-parent, two-child household with a breadwinner father and a stay-at-home mother—is nearly extinct. As one TV station put it: "Ozzie and Harriet are dead."

- One-quarter of our children live in single-parent families.

- Three-quarters of mothers with school-age children work outside the home.

- Unlike families in other Western industrialized nations, American parents are not guaranteed health care for their children, and families do not receive sufficient income supports to prevent them from falling into poverty.

The bad news is that our children are in trouble. **The good news is that doing something to help our children is just not that complicated.** Decent schools, affordable health care, and equal opportunity will definitely yield a productive, well-adjusted next generation. One calculation of the cost of alleviating child poverty is $44 billion—less than the annual tax breaks we gave to our wealthiest citizens in the 1980s. And what an investment:

- For the price of one prison cell, we can send 20 kids to college.

- For the price of one more police officer on the street, we can put 20 kids in Head Start.

- For the price of putting a family on welfare, we can give 20 kids tutoring and job training.

Our children need our help. They can't do it on their own. They need adults to give them the attention and affection that every child deserves, to protect them from danger, and to provide them with stable homes and a good education. They need adults to vote for politicians who will do right by kids.

THE CONCLUSION IS CLEAR: In failing our children, we fail ourselves.

Wherever we live across America, we have a stake in the fate of our children.

Everyone Can Help

It takes an entire village to raise a child.

—African Proverb

TODAY THERE IS A NEW SPIRIT of optimism and hope in the United States. We have an opportunity to capture that spirit on behalf of our children. If everyone who picks up this book carries out just *one* of its suggestions, the resulting groundswell of activity on behalf of children will reverberate throughout America. *Together*, all of our volunteer efforts and political acts will create the momentum that is needed to save our children and our country's future—and to change our own lives in the process.

As the director of a child advocacy organization in San Francisco, I have seen many small acts add up to big differences:

- The parent whose persistent letters, calls, and sudden appearances at City Hall kept the city from closing her local library.

- A volunteer who tutored a tough youth incarcerated in Juvenile Hall—a student who now goes to college instead of prison.

- The Girl Scout leader whose troop—from the mayor's elementary school alma mater—convinced the mayor to open playgrounds after school.

- The volunteer at the homeless shelter who leads weekend outings that provide a bright spot in the dreary shelter routine.

- The senior citizen at the community hearing whose simple arithmetic (expanding child care would only cost one cent per day per San Franciscan) humiliated the city bureaucracy into voting "yes" on child care.

- The employees of a local business who banded together to convince their employer to change his position on parental leave, so that their colleague could keep her job when she had her baby.

- The community activist who singlehandedly convinced local politicians to take action to reduce the sheer number of guns in the city when she stood outside City Hall surrounded by coffins representing children who had been shot in drug violence.

Things are changing: Witness President Clinton taking the time early in his administration to address the concerns of children. When I began my work 15 years ago, my organization was lucky to get several calls a year from interested citizens asking what they could do to help the city's children. Now we get several calls a day. Our experience reflects the mood of the nation: In a 1992 poll, 61% of Americans listed as one of their top priorities guaranteeing basic services to children—a full 14 points higher than their next choice.

Ordinary Americans—like you—have the common sense to know that we must turn things around *now*. Together, we have the power to say to every politician, every business leader, every agency administrator, "The days when you could turn your back on children are over." Together, we have the compassion to say to the children of America, "Every kid counts."

Supporting children can be good policy and good politics. If more people in America care more about children than about any other issue, our voices will be heard. Every Congress member receives only an average of 100 letters on any given issue. People who care about children can certainly manage that! Right now, the most powerful lobby in America is the one that lobbies for guns. Think how much more power the people who lobby for children could have.

Children are remarkably resilient. It often takes surprisingly little to change a child's life for the better. Many successful adults remember a pivotal experience that allowed them to turn their lives around: a single teacher who had confidence in them, a Big Brother who paid attention at a critical moment, a summer camp that broadened their horizons and changed their self-image, one safe place they could go after school, a friendly neighbor.

By picking up this book, you have already begun to say to all our children, "I will not let you down." Read on, and you will find the action that is right for you. Your *one* action, when combined with the actions of all your fellow Americans, will create a voice that is as urgent as the Environmental movement, as principled as the Civil Rights movement, and as close to home as the Women's movement. **You will become a part of the next great movement in America: the Children's movement.**

Finding Your Niche
in the Children's Movement

What can you offer the children of America? You may spend five minutes at your kitchen table writing the mayor about the state of your neighborhood playground. You may spend an hour a week reading and laughing with a needy child. You may send a kid to camp. You may

decide to inspire your colleagues at work to "adopt a school." Whatever you have to give, if it's more than you are doing now, it will help.

Read part 1, 31 Ways to Save Our Children, for information and ideas. Then read part 2, Reviewing the Basics, to learn more about the skills you'll need to be an effective volunteer, an effective donor, and an effective child advocate. To give you even more help, we've included a list of resources—organizations and publications—at the end of each chapter, and a phone list of important numbers you can post in your home for easy reference.

Remember—you already have what it takes to be an effective child advocate:

- You don't have to be an "expert." Children need attention from ordinary folks, and politicians depend on their constituents for votes.

- You don't have to spend money. Attention is the greatest gift you can give a child, and listening does not cost money.

- You don't have to be a "power broker." People who are in positions of power have to worry about holding on to their power. The average citizen has the freedom to stand up for children. The power brokers will follow *our* lead!

Start now.
There is no "one" way to help children. You may not have the temperament to volunteer in a preschool. That's okay. You may hate politics. That's okay too.

You can find what is right for you. We hope this book will get you started.

The First Five Minutes

TO GET STARTED, consider trying just one of the following actions to improve life for America's children:

- **Put an "Every Kid Counts" bumper-sticker on your car.** Use the one enclosed with your copy of this book, and thousands of people will see it. Creating a movement for children means letting people know you are concerned.

- **Memorize this fact and tell it to a friend:** American children are more likely to be poor, drug-dependent, pregnant, murdered, or incarcerated than children in any other industrialized country.

- **Call the White House public opinion line: (202) 456–1111.** Tell President Clinton what you think must be done for children. If you support an action he has taken, let him know. Public opinion has a greater effect on policy than anything else.

- **Buy a children's book for your public or school library.** Library budgets in most communities have been cut drastically. Find a book that you think could inspire a kid, perhaps a biography of one of your heroes or heroines, a tale about another culture, or a story about the problems of growing up.

- **Call the Children's Defense Fund 24-hour hot line: (202) 662–3678.** You will hear a message from this country's leading advocacy group for children about what is happening on the federal level related to children's issues, and what action is needed.

- **Give a teenager you know a copy of "Kids Say Don't Smoke,"** a powerful little book with stories and posters by youths themselves. It could save a life. To order, call (800) 722–7202.

- **Call the Campaign for Kids' TV: (301) 270–3379.** Request a free packet on monitoring the Children's Television Act. It's up to the public to watchdog federal legislation limiting TV advertising and upholding program standards for children.

- **Donate a used toy, musical instrument, art supply, or article of clothing to a day-care center or homeless family shelter.** Check out your attic, garage, or closet. An underfunded children's program could make good use of some of those items you haven't touched in years. (To find a shelter or day-care center, call United Way or simply look in the Yellow Pages.)

- **Learn something about child abuse:** Write to the National Committee for Prevention of Child Abuse at P.O. Box 2866, Chicago, IL, 60690. Request their free pamphlet on preventing child abuse and neglect.

- **Order a compelling video that will educate you and your friends about what's happening to our children.** *I Wish I Were a Princess*, narrated by Peter Coyote, will tell you more in 12 minutes than you might learn in a lifetime. It is a story of five children, told in their own words, that is both shocking and inspiring. To order, call Coleman Advocates for Children & Youth at (415) 641–4362.

EVERY KID COUNTS

PART 1

31 WAYS TO SAVE OUR CHILDREN

Chapter 1

Turn Off the Tube

TV is everywhere—in our homes, our schools, and our workplaces. We have organized our schedules, our personal interactions, and even our furniture around television.... Our children spend more time tuned into TV than they spend at school, or with friends and family. In fact, they spend more time watching TV than anything else, except sleeping!

—From *Talking with TV: A Guide to
Starting Dialogue with Youth,*
Center for Population Options

Know the Facts

Between the ages of two and five, the average child spends four hours a day watching TV. By the time this child graduates from high school, he or she has spent 19,000 hours in front of the tube and will have seen close to a million commercials. Clearly, it's critical that we teach children how to use television: how to analyze it, how to participate in it, how to ignore its stereotypes and manipulations.

Here are some good reasons to turn off the tube:

- **TV serves up violence.** Each year, the average child views 1,000 rapes, homicides, or other brutal assaults on TV. Cartoons show an average of 32 violent scenes per hour!
- **TV reinforces stereotypes.** Between 75% and 90% of all stars in children's shows are white males. Criminals often have foreign accents and non-Caucasian features, and teenage girls are interested in little other than boys, shopping, and looks.
- **TV is a money machine.** Children's advertising on TV is a $500 million market. Says *PTA Today,* "It's 7 A.M. as America's kid awakens on Ninja Turtle sheets. He rises, dons Superman underwear, a Dick Tracy T-shirt, and sits down to Nintendo breakfast cereal with his Simpsons book bag beside him." Is there any doubt that our children are prime advertising targets?

- **Many children's TV "characters" are really products.** Programs such as "Masters of the Universe" are actually full-length commercials for toys. The programs are often financed by toy companies, which cross-promote with other companies like Burger King. George Gerbner, of the Annenberg School of Communications, puts it succinctly: "Most of the stories [children] hear are not told by parents, the school, the church, or neighbors. They are told by a handful of conglomerates who have something to sell."
- **Watching TV is not healthy.** Children who watch lots of TV are learning passive behavior. They are more likely to be overweight and depressed than children who watch little or no TV.

What You Can Do
about TV Addiction . . .

Dragging your child away from the TV may seem hopeless, but it's not. Take a look.

. . . At Home

Turn the TV off.   Now you and your child can talk! Discuss what kind of day your child is having. When you turn the TV back on, watch it together. Discuss the merits of the program. Use TV to initiate discussions about values, sex, and relationships. Voice your own concerns and opinions, and listen to your child's ideas.

Teach critical thinking.   Help children become sophisticated TV critics by encouraging them to write reviews or to create a rating system for the programs they watch.

Demystify commercials.   Teach your child how to watch commercials. Talk about the techniques commercials use to manipulate viewers—including the music, the visuals, the people. Commercials, like bullies, are best handled by neutralizing their power.

Teach your child how to use a VCR.   Tape a selection of quality entertainment as well as educational programs, and let your children control the VCR. They'll soon learn that *they* have the power to control television, and to choose programs on the basis of merit. Encourage them to watch the entertainment and fast-forward through commercials.

Teach your child to make his or her own "TV shows" with a video camera.   When children approach TV as active participants rather than passive consumers, they soon learn that programming is a language they can speak as well as listen to.

Use TV to encourage reading.   Have your child look up unfamiliar words he or she hears on TV. Discuss characters and plots, and direct your child to similar characters or stories in books. Look for programming that relates to books, such as "Ann of Green Gables" and "Reading Rainbow."

. . . In Your Community

Become a TV watchdog for children.   Post the addresses and phone numbers of the major TV stations in your community (see the phone list at the end of this chapter and in the back of this book). Share your outrage when you see something offensive. Watch out for stereotyping, excessive violence, and ads that exploit children. This only takes a few minutes, but it can have a big impact!

You are not powerless. TV stations have modified programs in response to just a few letters. According to Fairness and Accuracy in Media (FAIR), only 12 calls to the sponsor of one sitcom was enough to get the sponsor to withdraw, and the show was eventually canceled. (Please remember to stay sensitive to First Amendment concerns. The goal is to increase education for kids, not to promote censorship!)

Help enforce the Children's Television Act. Thanks in great part to citizen-activist Peggy Charren, who launched a virtual one-woman crusade, Congress passed the Children's Television Act (CTA) in 1990. It limits commercial time in children's programming to 10.5 minutes per hour on weekends and 12 minutes per hour on weekdays (both still substantially more than what's allowed for adult programming). The act also mandates broadcast and cable operators to provide educational and informational programming. *Stations that are out of compliance with the CTA can lose their Federal Communications Commission (FCC) broadcasting license.* However, no one in the TV industry or the FCC seems to enforce the act, and TV stations try to fake compliance by ascribing educational value to such shows as "Super Mario Brothers." Here are some things you can do:

- Contact the Campaign for Kids' TV and the National PTA. They both have kits to help you guide your local efforts (see Resources).
- Watch TV on Saturday morning. Monitor commercial time and the ratio of "junk" programming to shows with educational and informational value.
- Call or write your local broadcasters to let them know that you're watching how well they are obeying the law, and that you know when they are up for license renewal. You can find this information in the kits mentioned above.
- Send letters and make phone calls to the FCC regarding station compliance and license renewal.
- Ask your local TV station about its plans for educational kids' programming. The law even permits you to see the station's files for children's programming. Share your views with the station manager.
- Get the video *It's the Law: How the Children's Television Act Can Make a Difference*, from the Center for Media Education, and show it to your local community organization (see Resources).

Organize an informal workshop on children and television. The Center for Media and Values (see Resources) has developed a package called *Parenting in a TV Age: A Media Literacy Workshop Kit on Children and Television.* This well-organized leader's guide will allow you to help yourself, your friends, and your neighbors become savvy counter-influences to television programmers and commercial producers.

Join the Public Debate: Fight Commercial TV in the Schools

Where but in the USA would educators consider delivering their captive audience over to advertisers of junk food and shampoos? Where else would self-respecting principals defend as enriching a daily TV program that is a cross between network news and MTV?

—From an editorial in the *Rocky Mountain News*

If you have not yet encountered Whittle Communication's Channel One, you will. It is a private enterprise that hopes to put its video program in classrooms all over America. The program gives each school $50,000 in video equipment in exchange for captive viewers from one of the hottest buying markets—our kids.

The Channel One program is a 12-minute simplified news show interspersed with two minutes of advertising for fast food, expensive sneakers, and other teen-targeted products. That's *one full school day per year* of advertising! The contract requires that teachers stop their lessons in order to watch the entire program, commercials and all.

Channel One is a glaring example of a frightening trend in American education—television commercial advertising and mandated, commercially produced curricula in the schools. Financially strapped schools are the most likely to be tempted by commercial offers. Not surprisingly, most education organizations strongly oppose commercial exploitation of the school curriculum. Says the president of the National PTA, "Our public schools must continue to be the marketplace for ideas, not a marketplace for profiteers."

Sooner or later, Channel One or some other type of commercial TV in schools will become an issue in your community. Fortunately, each individual school system can make its own decision. Here are some actions you might take:

- **Become informed** about Channel One and other types of commercialism in schools, and share this information with friends, colleagues, teachers, and children (see Resources).
- **Write or call the school superintendent** or school board in your community to let them know your objections to commercial TV in the schools.
- **Urge your local PTA** to oppose Channel One. Join the PTA (you don't have to have a child in school to do this) and offer to help with the campaign.
- **Write a letter to the editor** of your community newspaper opposing commercial TV in the schools.

Resources

Organizations

Campaign for Kids' TV
Center for Media Education
P.O. Box 33039
Washington, D.C. 20033-0039
(301) 270–3379
Public education project dedicated to maximizing the impact of the Children's Television Act. Ask for their information folder and video on monitoring the CTA.

Center for Media and Values
1962 S. Shenandoah Street
Los Angeles, CA 90034
(310) 559–2944
To order "Parenting in a TV Age: A Media Literacy Workshop Kit on Children and Television."

Federal Communications
  Commission (FCC)
Mass Media Bureau
1919 M Street, N.W.
Washington, D.C., 20554

(202) 632–7048 (complaint branch)
Call to protest noncompliance with the CTA.

National Coalition on Television
  Violence
P.O. Box 2157
Champaign, IL 61825
(217) 384–1920

National Education Association
  (NEA)
1201 16th Street, N.W.
Washington, D.C. 20036
(202) 833–4000
Find out about current actions in your state opposing Channel One in the schools; ask for their free booklet on watching TV with your children.

National PTA (see Multi-Issue
  Resources)
Ask for *The Children's Television Act: What Your PTA Can Do to Improve TV Programming*, and for information on Channel One.

National Networks: Children's Programming

Write or call the following regarding compliance with the CTA:

ABC Children's Programs,
   President
2040 Avenue of the Stars, 2nd Floor
Century City, CA 90067
(310) 557–6575

NBC Saturday Morning and Family
   Programming
NBC, Inc.
3000 W. Alameda Avenue
Burbank, CA 91523
(818) 840–3477

CBS Children's Programming,
   Vice President
7800 Beverly Boulevard
Los Angeles, CA 90036
(212) 975–3166

FOX Children's Network/
   Fox Kids Club
5746 Sunset Boulevard
Wilton Building, 6th Floor
Los Angeles, CA 90028
(213) 856–1800

PBS Director of Children's
   Programming
1320 Braddock Place
Alexandria, VA 22314
(703) 739–5000

Publications

The Plug-in Drug: Television, Children and the Family, by Marie Winn.
   New York: Viking Penguin, 1985.
The TV Smart Book for Kids, with
   pull-out parents' guide, by
   Peggy Charren and
   Carol Hulsizer.
   New York:
   E. P. Dutton,
   1986.

Chapter 2

Champion Public Education

If I told you that tomorrow America intends deliberately to take from our classrooms every third child and bury them alive, you'd gasp in horror. But we're already doing that. Twelve million young people are trapped in the debris of broken dreams.

—Bill Moyers

No nation has produced a highly qualified technical work force without first providing its workers with a strong general education. But our children rank at the bottom of most international tests—behind children in Europe and East Asia, even behind children in some newly industrialized countries.

—Commission on the Skills of the American Work Force

Know the Facts

"Not long ago," says NBC News anchor Tom Brokaw, "children starting kindergarten had a vocabulary of 4,000 words. Now many start with about a fourth of that." Every year, half a million teenagers drop out of school. Each year's "class" of school dropouts costs this country $240 billion in lost productivity and taxes over their lifetime.

School wasn't like this when I was a kid . . . Ironically, today's children require a higher level of education than ever before. Business leaders complain that the labor force cannot meet the skill level needed for expanding technologies. And the number of jobs requiring only minimum-level skill will be cut in half in the next ten years! According to a report by Workforce 2000, "Between now and the year 2000, for the first time in history, a majority of all new jobs will require postsecondary education." As John Sculley, CEO of Apple Computer, says, "We are trapped in an educational system that prepares youth for jobs that don't exist anymore."

A big problem is funding. The United States spends only one-third of 1% of the federal budget on elementary and secondary education. Japanese children spend 240 days in the classroom, in contrast to the 180 days American children spend. Lack of money means lack of resources:

- A high school teacher says: "I came into my classroom on the first day of school and had to send nine kids to the principal—I had 43 children in the class, and only 34 desks."
- A high school student says: "Our books are older than we are. And we can't even take them home to study. We have to leave them at school for the next class because there aren't enough."

What You Can Do to Save Our Schools . . .

. . . At Home: Help a Child

Read to a child. In *I Know Why the Caged Bird Sings*, Maya Angelou—the poet who read her work at President Clinton's inauguration—tells the story of a kindly neighbor who read to her from *A Tale of Two Cities*. This simple experience helped her regain her speech after the trauma of a childhood rape, initiated a lifelong love of language, and led to a renowned career as a writer.

Listen to a child read. The director of a tutoring program says, "The most effective role a volunteer can play with a child is to read and listen. This is a free gift—where ten minutes of your time equals ten hours of growth for a child."

Subscribe to a book club for a child. One woman remembers, "My aunt gave me and my sister a subscription to a children's book-of-the-month club when we were about eight. It was a glorious day when that book came in the mail. We listened to them being read, we read them again and again, and I still remember that wonderful feeling of owning our own hard-back books."

Get more involved in a child's school experience.   A child's chance of success in school increases greatly if a caring adult is involved. Help with homework, celebrate learning successes, and communicate with teachers.

Broaden a young girl's horizons.   Little girls are often given the message that they are not expected to achieve. When Mattel toys first made Barbie speak, for example, she said, "Math class is tough." Public outcry quickly made them drop this phrase. Make sure a little girl you know understands that the sky is the limit, and that you will support her along the way.

Become a volunteer tutor.   Tutoring is one of the most gratifying of all volunteer activities. One volunteer tutor felt great when he overheard his pupil's response to being teased for hanging out at the tutoring center: "I can't be just a football player," explained the youth. "I've got to have some smarts." Offer your tutoring services at your local school, library, PTA, volunteer center, or recreation program.

Volunteer to speak in a classroom or library program.   Everybody has a special topic to share with kids. Keep your talk short and fun. Give children a keepsake to take home and share with their families. For example, if you're speaking about birds, bring some feathers. The learning continues when the child brings the feather home and tells the family all about it.

Give a child a "First Day of School Kit."   A child's first day of school can set the tone for the rest of the year. Put together a book bag with pencils, pens, paper, erasers, and crayons or colored pencils for a child whose family can't afford it. Your local school, PTA, or community agency can help you identify a needy child.

Give a scholarship to prepare a kid for the future.   Perhaps the greatest gift a young person can receive is the opportunity for an education. The "donation" story of the decade is businessman Eugene Lang's spontaneous offer to a class of sixth-graders to pay for their college education. His commitment to this class of children resulted in the I Have a Dream Foundation, which now has sponsoring programs throughout the country. Call your local school district to find out about contributing to a scholarship fund, or start a scholarship in your name, or the name of someone you love.

Become a champion for public education.   Convince everyone you can—your dinner party companions, your work colleagues, your parents, your neighbors—that improving education is *everyone's* responsibility. People who say that education isn't their problem—"I don't have any kids," "Our kids are grown and have good jobs," "We send our kids to private schools where those problems don't exist"— need to reconsider their self-interest:

- 80% of our prisoners are people who never finished high school.
- The key to our security in the world is economic competitiveness, and a strong economy depends on an educated, productive work force.
- Anyone who plans to retire and collect Social Security in the next 20 years will be economically dependent on—that's right— the kids who are in school today.

. . . In Your Community: Improve Education

Stop the blame game.   We spend a lot of time pointing fingers about who's to blame for the sad state of education in America. Parents blame teachers. Teachers blame parents and funding. Kids say, "Nobody else cares, why should I?" Intercede whenever you see this happening, and try to focus attention on constructive solutions.

Visit a school.   How long has it been since you've seen the inside of a public school classroom? Make an appointment with the principal to take a "reality tour" of a local school. Once you have learned what it is really like, you can take your concerns to PTA meetings, local service clubs, or to your friends and neighbors. You will be one of the few members of your community who actually knows what's going on in the schools.

Donate books to the city or school library.   Budget cuts have severely curtailed library services in most communities, and donations are welcome. Consult with the librarian to select age-appropriate titles, and even posters, photos, and videos.

Write a tax-deductible check to your favorite school. No amount is too small or too large. You can sponsor a child who can't afford a field trip, underwrite playground equipment, or bring a performance. You can also support cash-register receipt programs at grocery stores that donate money or equipment (such as computers) to schools.

Write letters to school officials. Never underestimate the power of a letter. Most of us think of writing a letter when we are angry. But when you see something great happening in your schools, take a moment to write the principal, the teacher, or the school board to say that this is something you want to see continue.

Get involved with school-related boards and committees. Become an active voice at school board meetings, or join a parents' advocacy group or a school advisory committee. Work to elect school board members you can trust.

Support funding for public schools. Remind your friends that if they think education is expensive, they must consider the costs of neglecting it.

Join the Public Debate: Reform = Access + Relevance + HARD CASH

Everyone has an idea for saving America's schools. Some call it "restructuring" or "shared decision making" (giving teachers and parents a greater role in decisions is valuable, but no substitute for adequate resources); and some call for setting "national standards" (measuring our children may help us know how well they are doing, but it is not the same as educating them). Then there is the public-private partnership—the notion that corporations are going to bail out the schools. The donated computers are great, but they barely make a dent in the budget problems. **Beware of quick fixes!**

Eight Questions to Ask Yourself When You Evaluate the Next "Education Reform" Proposal

1. Will it give the underfunded schools more money and increase the per-pupil expenditure?
2. Will it give the teachers concrete resources (such as reductions in class size, more materials, field trips, the latest education technologies) to improve their skills and their classrooms?
3. Will it empower parents, students, and teachers to make education a more relevant experience; and does it promote teamwork between the school and the home?
4. Does it assure that more children will be "school ready" when they enter kindergarten?
5. Does it provide the schools with additional resources to address the many social problems children bring to the classroom, such as teen parenting, health, and nutrition programs?
6. Does it have hidden social costs, such as lack of equal access for all children?
7. Will more youth be job-ready as a result of the reform?
8. Is it based on a philosophy that all children be given the opportunity to achieve their full potential?

Support local innovation.   Schools don't have to be second-rate. Look for success stories and circulate them; you will often find them in the media. All over the country, individual principals, administrators, teachers, parents, school boards, and even students are initiating exciting reforms to improve education.

What About Vouchers?

The voucher system—publicly funded vouchers for public and private schools (this is not the same as the simple notion of parental choice within the public system)—is the most controversial educational issue of the decade. The National PTA expects vouchers to be on the ballot in ten states in the next two years. Here's how vouchers would work: Parents would get a voucher to pay for their child's education at the school of their choice—public or private. Sounds good on the surface, but there's more than one catch:

- **The most vulnerable children would be left behind.** Given the state of most public schools, many parents would choose to send their kids to private school. But vouchers would only pay for part of what most private schools charge, making these schools a vi-

"Oppose the voucher plan"

able option only for the well-to-do, and for few students from poor families who manage to get in on scholarships.

- **The public schools would deteriorate at the expense of the most vulnerable children.** All of the children who are now in private school at their parents' expense would be subsidized with government funds. This spreads education dollars among many more children, and dramatically reduces the per-pupil expenditure.

- **Vouchers could fund schools with biased curricula, discriminatory practices, and uncredentialed teachers.** Vouchers would provide public funding for schools that could exclude all types of kids—from the overweight kid who doesn't represent the school "image," to the child who doesn't speak English, to the teen mother who needs on-site child care. They undermine the separation of church and state by using public funds to promote a specific religion.

- **Applying free market concepts to schools does nothing to address the financial and social conditions that underlie poor education.**

Remember: We need to educate *all our children*. Public education is the bedrock of democracy.

Resources

Organizations

American Federation of Teachers (AFT)
555 New Jersey Avenue, N.W.
Washington, D.C. 20001
(202) 879–4596
Ask for information on school vouchers, Channel One, and other educational issues.

Americans United for Separation of Church and State
8120 Fenton
Silver Spring, MD 20910
(301) 589–3707
This watchdog organization, founded in 1947, opposes school vouchers.

I Have a Dream Foundation
330 7th Avenue, 20th Floor
New York, NY 10001
(212) 736–1730

National Committee for Citizens in Education
900 2nd Street, N.E., Suite 8
Washington, D.C. 20002–3557
(800) NETWORK
(800) LE AYUDA (Spanish)
Provides parents with information on public school issues, such as parent involvement, corporal punishment, suspension, special education. They give special attention to Spanish-speaking parents.

National PTA
(see Multi-issue Resources)
Send for their free catalogue on brochures, videotapes, planning kits, and books on a wide range of educational issues.

United Negro College Fund
500 E. 62nd Street
New York, NY 10021
(212) 326–1100

Publications

Crossing the Tracks: How Untracking Can Save America's Schools, by Anne Wheelock. New York: New Press, 1992.

Making Schools Better: How Parents and Teachers Across the Country Are Taking Action—and How You Can Too, by Larry Martz. New York: Times Books, 1992.

Parents' Guide to the Best Books for Children, by Eden Ross Lipson. New York: The New York Times, 1991.

Savage Inequalities: Children in America's Schools, by Jonathan Kozol. New York: Harper Perennial, 1991. A moving book on the status of public education in America today.

Save Our Schools: 66 Things You Can Do to Improve Education, by Mary Susan Miller. San Francisco: HarperSanFrancisco, 1993.

The Good Common School, by Joan First. New York: National Coalition of Advocates for Students, 1991. Addresses the need for fundamental school restructuring by defining ten critical student entitlements to make schools more responsive to the needs of all students. To order, call (617) 357–8507.

Chapter 3

Have Fun
with a Kid

Play . . . is the way a child learns what no one
else can teach him.

—Hartley and Goldenson,
The Complete Book of Children's Play

Know the Facts

In Navajo Indian culture, a child is watched over constantly until the
child laughs for the first time. This moment marks the child's birth as
a social being. The person who made the baby laugh then provides a
celebration in honor of the child.

Play is what kids do. It's how they test their limits, explore their in-
dependence, learn to work in a group, and—above all—have fun! But
for many children, the opportunity to play does not exist:

- Today's children are often passive and
  inactive as a result of the dramatic
  increase in television viewing
  and video games, combined
  with cutbacks in city-run
  recreation and physical education programs in schools.
- The "critical mass" of children
  needed for a spontaneous
  game of ball or hide-and-seek
  does not seem to exist in
  many neighborhoods. Many
  children are kept indoors—
  either because their neighborhoods are not safe, or
  because working parents

with children home alone want to know where their children are.

- Almost half of all children from low-income families do not participate in any organized extracurricular activities.
- Many girls lose out because of our male-oriented sports tradition. Only in recent times have girls even been allowed to participate in organized sports activities such as Little League.

What happens when kids don't play?

- Bored and isolated preteens and teens turn to vandalism, gangs, graffiti, violence, and drug abuse.
- Physical fitness declines: Childhood obesity has gone up 50% in the past ten years; and 55% of girls and 25% of boys can't do a single pull-up.
- Children get depressed. One in three teens today have considered suicide. Teen suicides have tripled in the past 30 years.

What You Can Do to Have Fun . . .

. . . At Home

Shhhhh! Learn to tolerate noise.   Fun is not quiet. Don't be a stick in the mud when kids are being expressive and ebullient on your block, in the park, or in your home.

Throw the ball! Throw the ball!   Call "time out" from your work to play. Did you know that today's parents spend 40% less time with their kids than parents 25 years ago? When a child wants to invite you into his or her games, join in. Whether it's a game of catch, hide-and-seek, or an invitation to the Mad Hatter's tea party, this is not the time to be shy or too busy with more "important" matters.

Make your home a place where kids come to have fun.   Sponsor a "Backyard Olympics." Kids love contests. You can provide hula hoops, jump ropes, or a badminton set, and reward the winners (and losers!) with some inexpensive prizes. Or string up some Christmas tree lights, pop some popcorn, turn on soul music, and have a "patio dance" for children of all ages.

. . . In Your Community

Donate games, toys, and arts and crafts supplies. Recreation centers, family shelters, and other community agencies must operate on desperately low budgets. Don't forget to participate in the annual "Toys for Tots" toy drive; purchase a new toy for a needy kid at holiday time.

Send a kid to camp. Sponsor a child who wants to go to summer camp or participate in an outdoor challenge course. You can do this through 4-H, Outward Bound, or any other outdoor program or camp in your area. There are even camps for kids with special needs. You can call United Way, religious organizations, Kiwanis, and even your local newspaper. The American Camping Association has a list of over 2,000 accredited camps. You can find their guide in your local library.

Lead a youth activity. Volunteer to teach arts and crafts at the local Boys and Girls Club, or coach a soccer team. Call one of the following organizations in your community and ask how you can help: American Youth Soccer Organization (AYSO), Camp Fire Boys and Girls, Girl Scouts of the USA, Little League Baseball, YMCA, and YWCA.

Help build or remodel a playground. Children's programs often build play yards primarily with parent and other volunteer support. As an alternative to conventional playgrounds, suggest that a day-care center or school consider building an "adventure playground." This is a great project, and something parents and kids can help build (see Resources).

Start a Midnight Basketball League. In 1987 G. Van Standifer, city manager of Glenarden, Maryland, initiated Midnight Basketball. The concept: Give young men the opportunity to engage in organized sports during the peak hours for criminal and drug activity—10 P.M. and 2 A.M.—and require them to participate in "life skills" workshops.

The best-known Midnight Basketball program is in the housing projects in Chicago, where it is the centerpiece of a program that provides comprehensive social and economic services (see Resources).

Become a playground "watchdog." When you see glass in the sandbox, broken swings or basketball hoops, drinking fountains that don't work, or recreation workers ignoring kids at your local park, don't just walk away. For the sake of all our children, call the director of your recreation department, someone on the city council, or even the mayor, and make sure they do something about it.

Join the Public Debate: It's a Whole New Ball Game

Cultural diversity can lead to recreational diversity. Many children living in America have come here from all over the globe, and bring with them experiences in all types of sports. Try to expand your ideas about what programs should be offered. For example, when schools offered soccer instead of basketball in a predominately Hispanic neighborhood in San Francisco, youth participation in recreation went from several dozen to 500 almost overnight!

Girls just wanna have fun! Pay attention to the needs of girls. Speak out when they don't get to participate. Demand that there be as many recreational activities for girls as there are for boys. Girls must have equal access to athletic opportunities and the educational and career benefits associated with participation in varsity sports.

Take on the "sacred cow" of competitive sports. Competitive sports are great, except when they become too aggressive or so important that kids lose perspective—which is all too often. Be one of those adults who raises the red flag when sports get out of hand.

Play some New Games. For an alternative to traditional sports and old attitudes about play, New Games promotes fun recreational activities that stress challenge rather than competition. Its motto is "Play hard, play fair, nobody hurt." Borrow from the library or purchase a copy of *New Games* and *More New Games* (see Resources).

Resources

Organizations

Midnight Basketball League
3628 Cousins Drive
Landover, MD 20785
(301) 772–1711
Call for information on starting a league in your community.

To Send a Kid to Camp
American Camping Association
5000 State Road 67N
Martinsville, IN 46151
(800) 428–CAMP (2267)
Call to order *Guide to Accredited Camps* ($10.95).

Girls and Sports
Girls Incorporated
30 East 33rd Street, 7th Floor
New York NY 10016
(212) 689–3700
Ask about how to start a Girls Club in your area.

National Association for Girls
    and Women in Sports
1900 Association Drive
Reston, VA 22091
(703) 476–3450
Ask for advice about laws requiring equal sports opportunities for girls; send for their *Title IX Tool Kit.*

Adventure Playgrounds
The Park People, Inc.
5615 Kirby, Suite 415
Houston, TX 77005
(713) 528–7725
Ask for *Where Do Children Play? In Adventure Playgrounds*, a manual on how to start an adventure playground.

Publications

Childswork, Childsplay. Free catalogue of games, books, records, and toys that address the emotional needs of kids. To order, call (800) 962–1141.

New Games, by the New Games Foundation Staff, edited by Andrew Fluegelman. New York: Doubleday, 1976.

Toys: Tools for Learning, by the National Association for the Education of Young Children. This brochure has tips for making wise toy choices for children birth through age eight. To order, call (800) 424–2460.

Day Care NEEDS You!

Chapter 4

Adopt a Child-Care Center

Every time my child calls me at work, I panic. Maybe this is going to be *the* time—you know—when something terrible has happened.

—Mother of one of America's 3.4 million latchkey children

Know the Facts

American families are changing—fast. Most mothers of young children are not at home during the day. They're joining the work force in record numbers, often because they have no choice. Today nearly 60% of women with children under age six are working outside the home, compared to only 12% in 1950. More than half of all mothers return to work before their child is one year old.

That's why decent, affordable child care has become so important: it allows parents to work, and it assures them that their children will be safe and well cared for. But finding good child care can be a nightmare—no matter where you live, no matter what your income. It's been estimated that half of all parents looking for child care either don't find it, or are uneasy about the care they have found. In one study, half of the mothers surveyed reported that during work hours they could not call their children or receive calls from them (even in an emergency).

- **Child care is expensive.** A single parent earning $18,000 per year spends an average of 25% of her income on child care for one preschooler.
- **Child care is scarce.** As many as one-third of children ages five to 12 have no one to greet them when they come home from school. These "latchkey" children don't just get bored and lonely—the lack of supervision leaves them vulnerable to drug abuse and crime.

- **Child-care workers are hard to find.** Nearly half of all child-care workers leave their jobs every year. Why? Because over 70% of this predominantly female work force earns an income below the poverty level—less than the average parking lot attendant. When measured against inflation, child-care wages have actually *declined* more than 20% in the last decade.
- **Child care needs public and private support.** Countries such as France and Israel offer preschool child care as a free, public program to all parents. Not in America. In 1992 even Head Start, our premier early childhood program, served only one-third of the eligible children—and only for half a day, nine months of the year. Middle-income families often fare the worst: they're not poor enough to obtain subsidies, and they're not wealthy enough to pay for good care.

What You Can Do to Ensure Quality Day Care . . .

. . . At Home

Learn how to identify good-quality care. Whether you're seeking care for your own child, or trying to find a program where you can volunteer or make a contribution, pay attention to these key ingredients:

- **The staff:** Are the caregivers well-trained? Do they seem warm, sensitive, and caring? Are they interacting with the children, or are they occupied with other things? What discipline methods do they use? Is there a good adult-to-child ratio? Do they communicate well with parents?
- **The children:** Are they playing freely and happily, or do they seem subdued, bored, or restless? Do they have a choice of activities and play areas, or is play rigidly structured?
- **The program:** Are the toys, art supplies, and books adequate and appropriate for the group? Does the staff plan a variety of activities each day? Is the program licensed? Have thorough emergency procedures been developed?

. . . In Your Community

Donate materials to a child-care center.   Save up paper at your office. Collect plastic bottles, scraps of material, "dress-up" clothes—use your imagination, and ask the center staff what they would like. One volunteer donor said, "As the children paraded around in the colorful hats and jackets and dresses, I could see that my Goodwill rejects were going to lead to hours of imaginative play."

Volunteer to help out at a child-care center.   Child-care centers are often short on staff, and volunteers—from teenagers to grandparents—can make an immeasurable contribution. As one parent said, "Talking to Grandpa Harry, the senior citizen volunteer, was often the highlight of our child's day."

Offer space.   Find out whether your church or synagogue, or any other group you belong to, can offer low-cost or rent-free space to a center serving low-income families. Did you know that churches are the major sponsor of child-care programs in America?

Subsidize a child whose parent can't afford care.   A "child-care scholarship" could be the best start in life a child receives. Consider donating to such a fund at your "adopted" center, or find the child-care voucher program in your community by calling the child-care resource and referral agency nearest you (see Resources).

Champion the cause of child-care workers. The key to quality child care is the training and skill of caregivers, but the field is continually losing its best workers because of poor wages and benefits. If you use child care, support good working conditions for caregivers. You might start by asking a child-care worker you know about his or her salary. You will be shocked! You can also help by joining the Worthy Wage Campaign, a growing national effort to solve the child-care staffing crisis (see Resources).

Encourage your employer to be child-care friendly. More and more companies, large and small, are finding that it's good business to help employees meet child-care and other family needs. Organize a group of friends at work to ask your bosses about their position on child-care issues, such as providing child-care information to employees. (See chapter 13 for details.)

Adopt a child-care center at your worksite. Encourage colleagues to attend the center's fundraiser, provide pro-bono bookkeeping, public relations, or other services, or volunteer.

Consider starting a child-care program in your home. If your house is a magnet for local kids, or if you would like to be at home with your young children but need to earn an income, consider operating a family day-care program in your home. Family day care is the most widely used form of child care in the United States, and home-based providers are finding that it's both a viable small-business opportunity and a rewarding profession (see Resources).

Join the Public Debate:
Make Child Care Safe and Affordable

Fight for public funding of child care. Public funding for child care is grossly inadequate. Even the much-heralded federal bill passed in 1990, the Child Care and Development Block Grant, will serve only some 400,000 children—fewer than 4% of the population under the age of six with working mothers. And even this small amount is in constant jeopardy at budget time. Let your legislators, and the local media, know that quality child care is not only a necessity—it's a sound investment in our children's future.

Make sure child care is regulated. Child-care regulations are in jeopardy in many states, as governors and legislatures attempt to cut back or eliminate the funding of licensing offices. Some states have more regulations governing animal care than child care! Support the call for local and national child-care quality standards. Children's health and safety are at stake.

Tell your child-care stories. End the conspiracy of silence. Spurred by the child-care controversies involved in finding the first woman Attorney General, columnist Ellen Goodman made the following plea:

> Now we are into the 90s. The two-worker family is the norm. But so is haphazard, uneven, inadequate child care. So are our worries. So is this silence. Our reticence to speak out may be due simply to pain. The fear that our children are hurt—whether by abuse or loneliness—may in turn hurt too much to talk about. It may be due as well to the lack of choices. To the lingering idea that child care is still, really, a mother's job.
>
> But at some point, we have to get off this silent defensive. We can only do that by speaking out. By sharing thousands of personal stories of ourselves and our children until we have made that click of recognition—I'm not the only one—that motivates change.

Resources

Organizations

Child-Care Action Campaign
330 Seventh Avenue, 17th Floor
New York, NY 10001–5010
(212) 239–0138
Offers public education and advocacy on child care. Ask for information on employer child-care support, finding quality care, liability insurance, and many other child-care issues. Send a self-addressed, stamped envelope for free information guide on selecting good child care.

Ecumenical Child-Care Network (ECCN)
National Council of Churches of Christ
Child and Family Office
Margery Freeman
1119 Dauphine Street, #5
New Orleans, LA 70116
(504) 522–9895
This group provides information for churches on church-housed child care.

National Association of Child-Care
Resource and Referral Agencies
P.O. Box 40246
Washington, D.C. 20016
(202) 333–4194
Ask for help finding the agency in
your area that offers child-care
referrals, information about employer
child-care support, voucher programs,
and other financial aid for parents.

National Association for the
Education of Young Children
(see Multi-Issue Resources)
This organizations is an excellent
source of training materials, posters,
brochures, and other information on
child care.

National Association for Family
Day Care
1331A Pennsylvania Avenue , N.W.,
Suite 348
Washington, D.C. 20004
(800) 359–3817
Ask for information on how to start a
child-care program in your home.

Worthy Wage Campaign
c/o Child-Care Employee Project
6536 Telegraph Avenue, Suite A-201
Oakland, CA 94609
(510) 653–9889
This is a five-year nationwide
campaign to address the critical
economic needs of the child-care
work force.

Chapter 5

Fight Childhood Poverty

> For ten generations American mothers and fathers left better-educated children a more competitive economy—until my generation. . . . My generation has turned the Bible on its head. We have become the prodigal parents. We are upwardly mobile. Our children are downwardly mobile.
>
> —Richard Lamm, former Governor of Colorado

Know the Facts

Look around you: **Poor children are everywhere.** Although they are concentrated in inner cities, over half of poor children live outside urban areas. One-third of all our children are eligible for government assistance because of their low income.

Children who live in poverty are hungry, worried about losing their home (if they have one), and can't do many of the things other children take for granted—like buy a popsicle, go to a movie, or even get a needed pair of new shoes. Poor children face a constant televised barrage of upscale families and advertisements for consumer products they cannot afford to buy.

Poverty kills children. It kills their pride, their hope for the future, and their bodies. Each day in America, 27 children die from the effects of poverty.

- Poor children are three times more likely to die from accidents and disease than children who are not poor.
- The United States has the highest child poverty rate of any country in the industrialized world—one in five American children is poor.
- In 1991 half of the new people who fell into poverty were children. Children are twice as likely as adults to live in poverty.

Families in poverty are not lazy: Sixty percent of poor families with children work at some time during the year. Half work year-round, full time, but low wages and frequent job loss keep them in poverty.

- In 1993 a family of four was considered poor if they had a cash income of less than $14,350.
- A person working full-time at the minimum wage will make only 65% of the poverty level for a family of four.

To LaJoe, the neighborhood had become a black hole. She could more easily recite what wasn't there than what was. There were no banks, only currency exchanges, which charged customers up to $8.00 for every welfare check cashed. There were no public libraries, movie theaters, skating rinks, or bowling alleys to entertain the neighborhood's children. For the infirm, there were two neighborhood clinics, both of which teetered on the edge of bankruptcy and would close by the end of 1989. Yet the death rate of newborn babies exceeded infant mortality rates in a number of Third World countries. And there was no rehabilitation center, though drug abuse was rampant.

—from *There Are No Children Here* by Alex Kotlowitz

Remember: Some experts say that the cost of significantly addressing child poverty in America would be no greater than the cost of bailing out the savings and loan disaster.

What You Can Do to Fight Poverty

Become a mentor to a needy child.

I have been able to give guidance and love to Jamar. When Jamar's cousins were killed by a gang, Jamar began to share his deepest fears with me—particularly his fear about being black and male. I'm not a substitute dad, nor an assigned mentor, but a true, honest-to-goodness friend.

—Big Brother to a 13-year-old boy

Three-quarters of the children in single-parent families live in poverty at some time during their first ten years. These children need a mentor, a caring adult who can do the simple yet enriching things that their parent alone may be too busy or overwhelmed to do. You can play in a park, or visit a public library. For many children of poor families, just spending time outside of their neighborhood can be an eye-opening experience. You can probably find at least one organization in your community that will link you with a child in need of a mentor (see Resources).

Sponsor a child. For as little as $20 a month, you can become a child's financial sponsor. Save the Children, the best-known national organization, will arrange for you to correspond with your sponsored child (see Resources).

If you'd prefer a more personal approach, why not invent your own child-sponsoring program? Find an organization in your community that serves low-income children—a day-care center, a family counseling program, a child-abuse service—and offer to sponsor a child in particular need. You can send the family (or the agency) a regular check for the child; send gifts and letters; or pay for a one-time important expense, such as back-to-school clothes.

Become an activist for parental leave policies. Many families cross the line into poverty when a single mother loses her job because her employer is unwilling to grant maternity or emergency leave. Fortunately for America's parents, one of President Clinton's first actions was to sign the Family and Medical Leave Act, giving employees of businesses with over 50 workers 12 weeks of guaranteed unpaid leave for the birth or adoption of a child and for the serious illness of a child, spouse, or parent. After seven years of discussion and two vetoes by

President Bush, the United States joined other industrialized countries in providing family leave benefits.

But the fight is not over. Inevitably, some companies will attempt to circumvent the law. Parents will have to demand their rights, and they will need the support of their coworkers. Also, most of the female work force is probably not covered by the law, since many women don't work in large companies. Finally, the law is extremely modest. In most Western European countries, leave is paid, and it is longer than 12 weeks. American parents have made a solid first step on family leave, but the struggle is hardly over.

Spread the word about tax benefits for poor families. Many low-income families do not know that they may be entitled to money back from the federal government. Fortunately, the Center on Budget and Policy Priorities has mounted a nationwide campaign to educate families about this potential benefit. To qualify, a person must have earned less than $22,370 from a job or self-employment, and have a child living with them for more than six months of the year. Give the information number to a parent you know who might qualify, or order the information brochure and post it on the laundromat or day-care center bulletin board. In 1992, a family could get a tax refund of up to $2,200. That's a lot of money for a low-income parent.

Remember: Child poverty will only be fully addressed when this country has economic policies that assure every family the opportunity for a decent income. This means an increase in the minimum wage, tax policies that guarantee a minimum standard of living for families, child-support assurance, adequate unemployment benefits, a federally funded training and jobs program, a competitive work force, and a flourishing economy.

Resources

Organizations

Big Brothers/Big Sisters of America
230 North 13th Street
Philadelphia, PA 19107
(215) 567–7000
Contact the national headquarters to find your local affiliate.

Christian Children's Fund
2821 Emerywood Parkway
Richmond, VA 23261
(800) 776–6767
Ask about how you can sponsor a child in the United States or worldwide.

Earned Income Credit Campaign
Center on Budget and Policy
   Priorities (see Multi-Issue
   Resources)
(202) 408–1080
Call to receive a free outreach kit
containing information sheets,
posters, and fliers.

Save the Children
54 Wilton Road
Westport, CT 06880
(800) 243–4075
Ask how you can sponsor a child in
the United States or worldwide.

Publications

*Outside the Dream: Child Poverty in
   America,* by Stephen Shales. A
   stunning photographic essay
   produced in collaboration with the
   Children's Defense Fund.
*There Are No Children Here: The Story
   of Two Boys Growing Up in the
   Other America,* by Alex Kotlowitz.
   New York: Doubleday, 1991.
*Within Our Reach: Breaking the Cycle
   of Disadvantage,* by Lisbeth B.
   Schorr. New York: Doubleday, 1988.
   An analysis of programs that work.

Chapter 6

Defend the Children's Safety Net

Lorena is a 28-year-old single mother supporting her two children through AFDC. Two years ago she worked at a $17,000-a-year night job at the post office. Her three-year-old son, Nathan, would go to sleep at 8 P.M. She would wake him at 10 P.M. to take him to the babysitter's, wake him again to get him out of the car, and then leave him with the sitter until 7:30 A.M. Soon he began wetting the bed. She tried to get on a different shift, but there were no openings. After months of this routine, Nathan stopped talking. Lorena decided she could no longer do this to her son, and quit her job.

She now finds herself living on AFDC. She does a juggling act between paying her phone bill and her utility bill. Rice and beans are the mainstay of her family's diet. They can't afford to buy toilet paper or toothpaste. When her son gets ill, Medicaid will not pay for liquid Tylenol. She knows she needs to move to a cheaper apartment, but she can't save the money for the first and last month's deposit. Unless she is evicted and becomes homeless, she cannot receive help from the welfare department for moving costs. She would like to find a job and get off welfare, but she rarely has money for transportation and child care to search for a job. On the rare occasions when she can get a ride, it is usually to go to a food pantry or to a thrift store to buy clothing for her children.

—"The Catch-22 of Welfare," from Campaign for a Fair Share

Know the Facts

Anyone who cares about children has an obligation to understand the debate about welfare, one of the most important children's policy issues of the decade. The real name for welfare is Aid to Families with Dependent Children, or AFDC. AFDC is the children's safety net, and perhaps the most hated program in the country.

Most people know almost nothing about welfare, yet almost 15% of America's children will depend on this public assistance each year. The popular belief is that welfare has failed, yet without welfare millions of American children would be starving.

STEREOTYPE: Most people on welfare are black families with "too many" kids.

TRUTH: **There are almost as many white welfare recipients as black,** and the number of children per family is no larger than the average for families in general.

STEREOTYPE: The "welfare queen"—the lazy woman who cheats the state—will only get off welfare if she has a "kick in the pants."

TRUTH: **Many welfare recipients actually work,** but they earn so little money that they still qualify for some aid. All physically able recipients are registered in job-search programs—and many more welfare recipients are banging at the door to get into job-training programs than there are slots available.

Furthermore:

- 70% of welfare recipients are children.
- The average welfare benefit is $4 per day, per person.
- Welfare benefits are on the average less than half the poverty rate.
- An average spell on welfare for a family is less than a year.
- AFDC benefits have *declined* 43% from 1982 to 1991.
- Welfare benefits comprise less than 1% of the federal budget and 2% (on average) of any state's resources.
- Welfare serves fewer than 60% of all poor children.

This is how people end up on welfare:

- They lose their jobs and can't find new ones.
- They get sick, can't work, and don't have health coverage.
- The only employment they can find is a minimum-wage job without health coverage and without subsidies for child care.
- The spouse who was working walks out and provides no financial help.

In other words, *it could happen to almost anyone!*

What You Can Do to Improve the Welfare System . . .

. . . At Home

Know the facts about welfare.   Tear out or copy the fact list you just read and carry it in your wallet. Every time you get into a discussion with a colleague or friend about poverty or welfare, consult the facts. The greatest barrier to sound national policies about children and welfare is ignorance.

. . . In Your Community

Reform your local welfare department.   Going to the welfare department to get desperately needed help for your children can be a stigmatizing, humiliating, painful process. If you have a few hours and want to do *one thing*, find out where the welfare department is in your community. Then, simply sit in the waiting room and observe. Does the staff treat people courteously? Do people have to wait for unreasonable periods? Is child care available? How would you feel if you were on welfare? If you are concerned and have ideas about what improvements need to be made, start with a call or letter to the director of the welfare department. If you don't get anywhere, send your letter on to the newspaper, the mayor, or a legislator (and don't forget to send a copy to the welfare director!).

Join the Public Debate: Be Skeptical About So-called Reform Proposals

In the coming decade, there will be proposals in every state and many in Congress to "reform" the welfare system for children. If they are like any of the proposals put forward to date, many of these so-called reforms will be nothing but punitive. They will use inflammatory language, appeal to our fears about the economy, and exploit myths of "rich" welfare recipients. When you evaluate a proposal, ask the following questions:

1. Does this measure help an undereducated person become more qualified for the labor market?
2. Does this measure provide more jobs? Does it guarantee a decent job to people leaving welfare?
3. Does this measure help poor families with child care and health

benefits, so that their children will be safe and cared for if their parents go back to work?

4. Does this measure help prevent homelessness, since many of the homeless are from AFDC families?

5. Does this measure make work pay—so that a person working at a full-time job can lift his or her children out of poverty?

Watch the media like a hawk.   Journalists play a powerful role in determining public opinion about welfare programs for children. If you think you see unfair coverage on the news regarding the homeless and poor, call the station. If you read a newspaper editorial endorsing welfare "reform" that is merely punitive, write a letter to the editor. Ask a columnist who generally supports women and children's issues to write a story dispelling the misconceptions of poverty and welfare.

Support positive welfare reform.   The current welfare system is not great: It does not put people back to work. It does not pull children out of poverty. All it does is ensure the bare minimum for families—and it doesn't do that very well. Leap on opportunities to support enlightened proposals. Earmarks of positive welfare reform to watch for include:

"Stop! Our spending priorities are killing our children!"

- tax policies that increase incomes of low- and middle-income families, such as a refundable tax credit for families with children;
- meaningful education and job-training programs for welfare recipients;
- public employment opportunities for welfare recipients that include health care and child care.

Remember: More than with any other children's issue, public policies regarding welfare will depend on the attitudes of mainstream America. *You* have a critical role to play in molding these attitudes. Many countries, including Holland, Germany, Denmark, Sweden, France, and Canada, already have social safety nets that prevent poverty and promote education and training.

Resources

Organizations

Center on Budget and
Policy Priorities
(see Multi-Issue Resources)
Ask for information on the welfare system.

Children's Defense Fund
(see Multi-Issue Resources)
Ask for information on child poverty and policy options to end child poverty.

Publications

Poor Support: Poverty in the American Family, by David T. Ellwood. New York: Basic Books, Inc., 1988.

Chapter 7

Help a Child Avoid Having a Child

I wanted somebody who would love me for myself.

—Teen mother talking about why she had a baby

When a young teenager has a baby, her life and her opportunities change forever. She hopes to find comfort and love. Instead, she is overwhelmed by the demands of a needy child. She is isolated from her friends, and often no longer in contact with the child's father. She is usually unable to finish school or get a decent job. More than likely, she lives in poverty. This is a tragedy for the mother, the child, and the rest of us who counted on this teenager achieving her full potential.

Know the Facts

Our children are having sex at an earlier and earlier age—more than half of our teenagers are sexually active. This shouldn't surprise us. Teens are exposed to daring sexuality—on TV, in movies, in magazines, and by advertisers as a marketing tool—on a daily basis. Ironically, curious teens generally do not have access to the straightforward information about sex that they need.

- Almost 3 million teens are infected with a sexually transmitted disease each year.
- America has the highest rate of teen pregnancy and childbearing of all developed countries in the world.
- One out of every five babies born in the United States is born to a teenage mother.
- Two-thirds of teen births occur outside marriage—a percentage that has more than doubled in the past 20 years.
- Half of the women currently on welfare bore children as teenagers.

What's wrong with this picture? Between 1980 and 1990, the decade of the greatest reported increases in adolescent birthrates, total public expenditures for family planning declined by one-third. Yet the annual cost to the taxpayer to assist families that began with a birth to a teen is $25 billion!

What You Can Do to Prevent Teen Pregnancy . . .

. . . At Home

Be an "askable" adult.   Many young people never talk to any adult about sex and contraception because both the child and the adult are uncomfortable with the subject. Share your values about personal responsibility and relationships in a way that invites discussion and openness. Talk about how having a baby so early in life can get in the way of achieving personal dreams.

A condom-carrying crusader: one woman's mission . . .   One dedicated child advocate, deeply concerned about teen pregnancy and the spread of sexually transmitted diseases, regularly carries a brightly colored condom key chain. She finds that people ask her about it all the time—strangers in the supermarket line, parents at her son's basketball practice, kids in the car pool. She says that it is a great way to get people to talk about AIDS and sexual responsibility—ordinarily tough subjects to broach.

Support healthy choices.   Teens who are not sexually active need support in their decision. They are often under a great deal of peer pressure. Be supportive of individual kids you know, and of activities and organizations in your community that give adolescents viable alternatives to early sexual activity.

Pay attention to girls!   The needs of teenage girls are frequently overshadowed by the needs of adolescent boys—who often get into trouble on the streets as a signal for help. Be aware that your own daughter may feel less important than her brothers, or than the boys in school. Consider volunteering for a program that provides girls with role models. Girls need to know that getting pregnant isn't the only way to gain recognition.

Teach boys that sex is not a conquest. Candid discussions can help our young men learn that they don't have to have sex to prove themselves. Be a role model—either as a parent, a relative, or a volunteer.

. . . In Your Community

Support family planning education in the schools. "I didn't know I was pregnant until I was four-and-a-half months along," says a 14-year-old mother. "I started my period when I was 13, and I got pregnant six months later. When my period didn't come, it didn't register. I thought that when you got pregnant, you showed a big belly right away. Then automatically you'd know."

Kids today need to learn a lot more in school than algebra. Check out the program (or the lack of a program) in your local school system. Support a comprehensive curriculum that helps teens make the right personal choice, and make sure that information about family-planning clinics is available as part of the course. Speak out about how important it is for teens to learn about sex.

A success story . . . Three years ago one school in eastern Arkansas had a 57% pregnancy rate. Then they instituted a school-based clinic. In the three years it has been there, *they have not had a single pregnancy, abortion, or dropout.* This is a school where 97% of the children are on welfare. We can teach children, and we've got to.

Support school-based health services. One of the most innovative ways to prevent teen pregnancy is to put health services at school sites. Teens are so wary of seeking health care and so good at denial that unless the health services are right in their own backyard, they will not use them. In some high schools, health workers not only have regular hours in a clinic, but they hang out in the cafeteria, in front of the school, and in other places where they can talk to kids informally and encourage them to use clinic services.

Remember: Given the increasing number of adolescents at risk for HIV/AIDS (see chapter 24), and the lengthy period of incubation (which indicates that many people become infected while they are still adolescents), it is imperative to coordinate AIDS prevention and adolescent pregnancy prevention efforts.

Get family planning information to teens. Most teenagers wait almost a year between becoming sexually active and making their first visit to a family-planning clinic. Many finally go to a clinic only to con-

firm that they are pregnant. Sexually active teens who aren't pregnant need help not only in finding which clinic to use for services, but constant encouragement to use birth control methods effectively once they have received them.

- **Ask young people what they know about existing services.** Do they know where to go if they want birth control or help if they become pregnant?
- **Urge local agencies to make information available to teens.** Use the information you got from the teens to lobby local agencies, schools, and your county health department to make information more accessible to youngsters through brochures, posters, outreach in schools, and so on.
- **Display educational posters and brochures.** Pregnancy prevention posters send powerful messages to teens to avoid pregnancy—for example, "Getting pregnant is like being grounded for 18 years." Order from the Children's Defense Fund (see Resources), and put them in your church, school, community center, or shopping mall. Contact your local family planning agency and ask if you can write their phone number for information at the bottom of each poster. Do the same thing with family-planning educational brochures.

Help a pregnant teen or a teen parent.   Pregnant teens who are lucky enough to get into teen parent programs can usually stay in school or get job training. These programs provide child care, health services, and counseling, and have been effective in preventing a second pregnancy. Offer your services to an organization in your community (such as Florence Crittenden or Family Service Agency).

A caring adult can make a difference . . . One volunteer with a teen mothers' program recalls, "I decided to teach the girls in a teenage parent center how to crochet. It was an amazing experience. Here was Jane, flunking out of school, always late to the center classes, not getting along with the other girls, and due in three months. It wasn't easy for her, but she learned the stitches and was able to make a coverlet for her baby. I think it was one of the few times in her life she had mastered a skill. And we both felt great!"

Schedule a parent education workshop on teen pregnancy. Many parents know very little about contraception and how to talk to teenagers about sex. Call a community agency—such as Planned Parenthood, the local health department, or an AIDS-prevention program—and schedule a parent education workshop at a school, worksite, child-care center, or in your home. Parents can become excellent family-life teachers.

Join the Public Debate

Join a local network or agency (such as the Junior League, Association of American University Women, or church groups) that is working on the issue of teen pregnancy. One coalition of adolescent pregnancy prevention advocates printed hundreds of pink and blue "birth announcements," each highlighting one teen birth, giving the baby's sex and weight, whether it was premature or not, and the ages of its parents. They filled a cradle with the announcements and called a press conference to bring attention to the problem.

If you are pro-choice . . . This is a treacherous time for teenagers who may choose to have an abortion. One of the most controversial issues is whether teens need parental permission to have an abortion. On the surface this sounds like a benign idea—it might even foster a closer relationship between parent and child. In the ideal situation, it might. Unfortunately, for many pregnant teens the ideal situation does not exist. Rather than face parental rejection and abuse, teens have been known to inflict injury on themselves, attempt to have illegal and unsafe abortions, or bear children they cannot care for. Call Planned Parenthood, NOW, or the National Abortion Rights Action League to get involved. Teens need confidential and legal services.

Resources

Organizations

Center for Population Options
1025 Vermont Avenue, N.W.,
    Suite 210
Washington, D.C. 20005
(202) 347–5700
Provides advocacy training and technical assistance to youth-serving agencies, policy makers, media, and other individuals on issues related to adolescent sexuality and pregnancy.

Children's Defense Fund
    (see Multi-Issue Resources)
Ask for information, posters, advocacy materials; CDF has made teen pregnancy prevention a major focus of its work.

Family Life Information Exchange
P.O. Box 37299
Washington, D.C. 20013-7299
(301) 585–6636
This is a clearinghouse for information on adolescent pregnancy and family planning. Send for free brochures.

National Urban League
Youth Resources Program
500 East 62nd Street
New York, NY 10021
(212) 310–9000
Ask for fact sheets, mentoring kit, posters, videotapes.

Planned Parenthood Federation
    of America
810 Seventh Avenue
New York, NY 10019
(212) 541–7800

Publications

*Adolescent Pregnancy Prevention,
    A Guidebook for Communities,*
    by Claire D. Brindis. Palo Alto, CA:
    1991. Stanford Center for Research
    in Disease Prevention. To order, call
    (415) 723–0003.

ETR Associates/Network Publications
P.O. Box 1830
Santa Cruz, CA 95061-1830
(408) 438–4060
Free catalogue of health education materials, pamphlets, and videotapes.

Chapter 8

Do Something About Child Abuse

I want my mom to stop whuppin' me. She won't let me tell anyone, she'd whup me more. I like to be here at the day-care center. That's why I come every day. I feel safe here. If somebody pick me up, I ask my mommy, can I spend the night, and never go back home no more.

—Charlene, age 6

Know the Facts

Child abuse has been around the human community for a long time. The fact that we're hearing about it more often means we're finally emerging from generations of silence.

What we know about child abuse is chilling. We know that child abuse is often a learned behavior handed down from one generation to the next. We know that, given the wrong circumstances, *nearly anyone* could abuse a child. And we know that the most likely place an American child will first experience violence is in his or her own home.

- Child abuse occurs in all socioeconomic, religious, and ethnic sectors of our society.
- In 1992, 3 million child abuse reports were filed in the United States, triple the number in 1980.
- Children who grow up in violent homes come to believe that violence is a normal and acceptable way to control others. Most violent adults who are now in prison learned violence at home.
- The majority of abused children come from households where the mother is also abused and unable to protect her children from witnessing or experiencing violence.
- Child sexual abuse is an act of violence that often occurs in tandem with physical violence. Many experts estimate that one in four girls and one in seven boys will be sexually abused in some manner by the time they are 18.
- Every day in the United States, three children die as a result of abuse.

What You Can Do to Prevent Child Abuse . . .

. . . At Home

Give a parent a break.   Children don't hand their parents a how-to manual at birth, but our society still tends to expect families to "go it alone" and raise their children without anyone's assistance. Raising a child is tough! *All* parents need help, and many parents—those who are isolated from their family or community, or who are young, or who are having financial or marital problems or other stresses, or who were raised by inadequate or abusive parents themselves—need extra help. You can help a child by offering to help a parent: Offer to baby-sit or share grocery-shopping and other chores; lend an ear and show you understand what parents go through.

Know the warning signs.   If you spend much time around children, you should be aware of signs that *may* indicate physical or sexual abuse. Look for patterns, not isolated incidents.

- **Physical abuse.** Children typically hurt themselves accidentally on the elbows, knees, chin, nose, forehead, and other bony areas. Bruises and marks from abuse, however, typically occur on other parts of the body: the soft tissue of the face, back, buttocks, arms, legs, or genitals. Head injuries are the most common cause of child-abuse–related deaths.
- **Sexual abuse.** A sexually abused child may have difficulty walking or sitting; torn, stained, or bloody underclothing; pain, swelling, or itching in the genital area; pain when urinating or defecating; bruises, bleeding, or lacerations in the external genitalia, vaginal, or anal areas; a vaginal or penile discharge; a sexually transmitted disease; or even a pregnancy.
- **Emotional abuse.** An emotionally abused child may experience speech disorders or lags in physical development, and may show a failure to thrive or a sallow, empty facial appearance.

Each of these types of abuse may also be accompanied by *behavioral* signs that range from depression, excessive clinging, or intensely negative attention-getting behavior, to isolation, destructiveness,

withdrawal, self-destructive or suicidal behavior, delinquency, running away from home, or alcohol or drug abuse.

Don't ignore trouble.   If you feel a particular child is being abused, don't jump in feet first. Be sure to proceed with caution, and don't draw conclusions too quickly—above all, avoid any harshness that could humiliate the parent and make the situation worse.

You might be able to strike up a conversation with the adult to direct attention away from the child, to show sympathy with the parent, or to offer some support—for example, "Grocery shopping with the kids is rough, isn't it? Is there anything I can do to help?" Or you might talk directly to the child to try to stop the child from provoking the parent—"I bet you're tired and you want to go home, don't you?"

If you know the parent, offer to watch the child while the parent takes a break. If you are concerned about the child's physical safety, you might need to take further action: If you are in a setting where there is someone in charge, such as a manager or playground supervisor, seek that person's help.

Report a reasonable suspicion of abuse.   All 50 states now require professionals who come into contact with children to report suspected child abuse to the proper authorities. But ordinary citizens really have this responsibility too. While different states have different procedures, making a report generally involves calling your local child protection agency. To find out what the procedure is for your area, call the toll-free National Child Abuse Hot Line number (see Resources). Reports are kept confidential, and require only a reasonable suspicion that needs to be investigated, *not* absolute proof of abuse.

. . . In Your Community

Help educate your community.

- Order child-abuse prevention posters, brochures, and fact sheets from national organizations (see Resources) and disseminate them in your community. (April—National Child Abuse Prevention Month—is an ideal time!)
- Urge your local radio and TV stations to broadcast public service announcements on the problem.
- Contact your local child-abuse council and invite a speaker to inform your PTA, church group, or other organization about solutions to the problem.

Volunteer at a child-abuse hot line.   Many communities now have switchboards that parents can call when they are feeling frustrated, angry, and at risk of taking it out on their children. These hot lines are often staffed by volunteers, who are given training in counseling, nonjudgmental listening, substance abuse problems, and child development. The work can be very gratifying.

> A very distraught father called our parental stress talk line. He had freaked himself out by spanking his seven-year-old boy so hard that welts showed. He had always used spanking as a form of discipline, but this time he felt he had lost control. I told him that all parents get angry at their kids, but acknowledged that it is really scary to feel out of control. I connected him with a parents' group and sent him some materials on discipline. I told him I would check back in a week. When I phoned back, he told me how the experience had brought back memories of his being spanked as a kid. He wanted to do better by his son. He thanked me for listening and not judging him.
>
> —Hot line volunteer

Oppose corporal punishment in the schools.   Many states and communities still allow teachers to strike children as a form of discipline. Most professionals consider this practice not only ineffective, but abusive. Find out the policy of your local school system, and initiate efforts to forbid teachers to hit their students under any circumstances.

Protest media exploitation of children.   Some forms of child sexual exploitation are actually promoted by the media and by the advertising industry—for example, using child models in ways that are intended to be sexually seductive. If you see such advertising, contact the newspaper or magazine editor or the TV station manager to insist that it be discontinued.

In December 1983 *Harper's* magazine ran a photo essay by photographer Francesco Scavullo called "Tiny Treasures," featuring a five-year-old girl promoting Chanel No. 5, Nina Ricci, Shalimar, and Estée Lauder perfumes. The copy referred to "seduction with just a hint of innocence." A public outcry led to apologies from the magazine and the perfume companies.

Remember: You can help break the cycle of child abuse—in one family, in one school, in one community. Don't turn away.

Resources

Organizations

National Committee
    for the Prevention of
    Child Abuse
332 South Michigan Avenue,
    Suite 1600
Chicago, IL 60604
(312) 663-3520.
(800) 835-2671(for publications
    only)
Ask for information and free materials
on parental stress and child abuse;
they have a comprehensive catalogue.

Parents Anonymous
(800) 775-1134
Call for a referral to a support group
for stressed parents.

Switchboards

National Child Abuse Hot Line
(800) 4-ACHILD
(Run by Child Help USA)
Call for information on how to report
child abuse.

National Clearinghouse on Child
    Abuse & Neglect
Department of Health &
    Human Services
(800) 394-3366
Free materials.

Chapter 9

Include Children with Disabilities

What bothers me the most—and it hurts me a
lot—is when people feel pity for me. My advice
to people who meet someone like me is to treat
them like a normal human being.

—Michelle, born without a hand,
from Jill Krementz,
How It Feels to Live with a Physical Disability

Know the Facts

Pity and avoidance are the most common responses to children with
disabilities. These responses are hurtful for both parent and child. As
one parent of a child with disabilities explains, "The ugliness [is] not
the individual with the disabilities; the ugliness is the picture of isolation, it is the despair, the hopelessness, it is the result of fear."

Families who have a child with disabilities face medical problems,
cultural stigmas, and financial nightmares and isolation. Fortunately,
these children have rights. The 1990 passage of the Americans with
Disabilities Act was a landmark step in ensuring services, equal opportunity, and accessibility to people with disabilities.

This is what "accessibility" means for children:

- If you can't walk, you can take the bus to school because it
comes equipped with a wheelchair lift.
- If you can't hear, you can still enjoy the children's theater performance because it's translated into sign language.
- If you can't see, you can still giggle with friends over the latest
teenage love story because the book is printed in braille.

This is what "full inclusion" means for children:

- A deaf child takes part in all classes—with the help of a sign language interpreter.
- A child who needs physical therapy receives those services during
the school day so she can attend regular classes.

- A child with learning disabilities stays in the classroom and receives special help.

We must work to assure that federal law is being enforced, and that attitudes change along with policies and architecture. Many school districts still shunt children with disabilities into "special" classes or schools. Children with disabilities may need special services, but segregation is rarely necessary. It often results in isolation, higher costs, inferior education, and the perpetuation of harmful attitudes. Families and children must be given options.

What You Can Do to Help a Child with Disabilities . . .

. . . At Home

Help individual children and their families. Here's the easiest—and possibly most helpful—idea in this book: The next time you see a child with disabilities, say "Hi!" One parent explains, "Very often when people see my daughter, all they see is her disability. They see her wheelchair, the way her eyes don't focus, the way she tilts her head. People don't say 'Hi' to her like they do to my other children. She is not only treated as stupid, but also as if she has no feelings. . . . Children with disabilities not only have feelings, but they learn about life by how people treat them, just like other children."

Offer help to a family with a disabled child.   If you know someone who has just given birth to a child with disabilities, be a friend and listen. Don't be afraid to hold the baby. Take an older child out for ice cream or to the park to give the family a break. Offer to stay with the child while they go out to dinner or spend time with their other children.

Volunteer to be with a child with disabilities.   Children with disabilities are inundated with people who are trying to "fix" them. For some it would be a pleasure just to hang out and talk! To volunteer, call your local United Way or one of the groups listed in Resources at the end of this chapter.

Talk to your child about children with disabilities.   First, listen to Krystle, age six, who has an artificial leg:

> Some of the kids at school called me "robot leg." . . . Mommy took me to my classmates' homes and told their moms that she didn't want them calling me names. Now they treat me differently. They protect me and look after me.

> —From Jill Krementz, *How It Feels to Live with a Physical Disability*

When you talk to your child, or other children, make the following three points clear:

1. **Children with disabilities may not be able to do some things,** but there are things a nondisabled child can't do either.
2. **Don't be afraid to talk to a child with disabilities.** Treat him or her as you would anybody else. People are different in many ways—skin color, hair color, right- and left-handedness. A disability is another difference.
3. **Use common sense about "helping" people with disabilities.** For example, if you see a blind child with a cane at a crosswalk, *ask* her if she would like some assistance in crossing the street. Don't just grab her by the elbow and steer her! If you want to communicate with a deaf child and can't talk sign language, try writing things down.

. . . In Your Community

Help change attitudes—your own included.

- **Educate yourself.** Order free information from the National Information Center for Children and Youth with Disabilities.
- **Speak up!** Why does it always have to be a person with disabilities, or the parent of a child with disabilities, who speaks up at a Boy Scout meeting or a church event and says, "Hey, how are we going to make sure kids with disabilities have access?" It could be *you.*
- **Learn the basics of signing.** In just a few minutes, you could learn how to greet a deaf child. Signing is fun, and a gift to yourself and others. Teach your own child—hearing children love to learn sign language.

Increase accessibility in your community—it's the law! Although the Americans with Disabilities Act requires that people with disabilities have reasonable access to all places, events, and other opportunities open to the public, compliance with this groundbreaking law will be spotty at best for many years to come. Here's what you can do:

- **Learn about the law.** Insist that it be obeyed. Report violations to the U.S. Department of Justice (see Resources).
- **Never** park in blue curb cuts or blue "handicapped" zones.
- **Talk to your local day-care center.** Encourage the director to offer care to children with disabilities. It's *very* difficult for parents of a child with disabilities to find care.
- **Fight for full access to neighborhood recreation programs.** Recreation is the perfect time for children with and without disabilities to socialize. Children with disabilities can play sports too, if the game is modified to accommodate their needs. Talk to program leaders and community officials.

Remember: The earlier you help children with disabilities, the more time they have to practice the skills that will make them productive adults, and the less cost to society in the long run.

Resources

Organizations

Association for Persons with
Severe Handicaps
11201 Greenwood Avenue N
Seattle, WA 98133
(206) 361–8870

Disability Rights Education
and Defense Fund
2212 6th Street
Berkeley, CA 94710
(510) 644–2555
This group provides advocacy
services.

Federation for Children with
Special Needs
95 Berkeley Street, Suite 104
Boston, MA 02116
(617) 482–2915
This information center for parents
of children with special needs also
provides referrals for local programs.

National Information Center for
Children and Youth with
Disabilities
P.O. Box 1492
Washington, D.C. 20013
(800) 999–5599
(703) 893–6061
(703) 893–8614 (TDD)
This is a federally mandated
information clearinghouse. Call for
free information for parents,
educators, caregivers, advocates, and
others; ask for referrals to local or
specialized organizations.

Special Olympics
1350 New York Avenue, N.W.,
Suite 500
Washington, D.C. 20005-4709
(202) 628–3630
Ask about competitive sports for
children with disabilities.

U.S. Department of Justice
Civil Rights Division
P.O. Box 66738
Washington, D.C. 20035-6738
(202) 514–0301 (voice)
(202) 514–0383 (TDD)
Call the ADA information line and
listen to an extensive tape with
information on all aspects of the law.

Publications

A *Difference in the Family*, by Helen
Featherstone. New York: Penguin
Books, 1981.
After the Tears, by Robin Simon.
Harvest Books, 1987.
*How It Feels to Live with a Physical
Disability*, by Jill Krementz. New
York: Simon and Schuster, 1992.
Poignant, yet uplifting, portrayal of
12 children whose disabilities
include paralysis, spasticity, and
dwarfism.
How It Feels to Fight for Your Life, by
Jill Krementz. New York: Firestone,
1993.
The inspiring stories of 14 children
who are living with chronic illness.

Chapter 10

Keep a Child's Creative Spirit Alive

I'm just experimenting. I'll come up with something eventually . . . It's really fun to make something nobody's ever seen before.

—A student absorbed by popsicle sticks and milk cartons at the Scrounger's Center for Reusable Art Parts (SCRAP) in San Francisco

Know the Facts

Young kids are vibrant with creative energy. They sing and make up songs, they dress up and create plays, they color, draw, skip, and do cartwheels. But too often their creative spirit dies at a very young age. Why?

- Many kids living in poverty lose the spark because they're just plain depressed—life comes down on them hard.
- The lure of electronic games and TV, combined with isolation and the lack of encouragement and freedom to be expressive, deadens the imagination and hope of many children.

Our challenge is to protect and nurture that precious, bright-eyed wonder of early childhood. The intense vitality of play and fantasy and expressiveness that you see in most kids is the spark of hope for a better tomorrow.

Imagination is more important than knowledge.

—Albert Einstein

What You Can Do to Promote Creativity . . .

. . . At Home

Give kids the freedom and encouragement to be creative. Appreciate and be involved when your kids are experimenting and expressing themselves—even if it's noisy and messy. Stop being judgmental—there are no right or wrong paths to creative discovery.

Give kids toys that encourage creativity.   Old standbys like Lincoln Logs and Legos are terrific. Avoid high-tech toys that encourage passivity.

Remember your own young creations.   Once upon a time we were all children—this makes us all potential experts! Try to remember the creative games and activities from your own childhood. You have a wealth of ideas stored inside, and they have stood the test of time. You can now pass them on to all our children.

One memory from my childhood is that a week after Christmas a friend and I gathered all the discarded trees from the alley and set up a Sherwood Forest in our backyard. The forest was the setting for unending episodes of Robin Hood, until my parents decided it was time to deal with the disposal problem. Such modern-day Sherwood Forests could be the object of a neighborhood tree recycling project.

Make an "imagination box."   Give the gift of imagination to a child you know, or to a day-care center, recreation center, or homeless shelter. One child advocate in San Francisco, unable to donate money, decided to create an "imagination box." She collected things all year— scraps of interesting fabric, bric-a-brac, toilet paper rolls, pictures cut from a magazine, anything that caught her fancy—and put them in a box. At the end of the year, she wrapped the box and presented it to a day-care center as the raw material and inspiration for free-wheeling creative projects. You could also put together a "theater in a trunk" filled with old clothes, hats, cast-off costume jewelry, and masks.

Pass on a very large box to a child.   After you purchase a major appliance, recycle the box to a child. You'll soon discover it's not a box at all, but a castle, a boat, an airplane, a jungle-gym—you name it, the opportunities for creative play are endless.

. . . In Your Community

Create a "culture kit."   Share your cultural heritage or unique interests with children. Put artifacts, photographs, puppets, travel posters, tapes, instructional materials, and so on together to donate or loan to a school or youth organization.

"Giddyup, giddyup"

Donate a musical instrument. School music programs are considered "frills" today and are desperately underfunded. If you have an instrument languishing in a garage, put it in the hands of a young student. Your local school's music department will be delighted!

Donate scrap paper. Underfunded day-care programs and schools often can't afford to buy paper for creative projects—especially heavier weight, colored, and specialty papers. Collect the paper that accumulates in the copy room and by the paper-cutter. Solicit donations by leaving a box at a local print shop or office and collecting it on a regular basis.

Send children to a concert, a play, or a museum. Donate tickets or pay admission fees for a cultural event children might enjoy. You can do this for individual children you know, or for a school class or youth group. Encourage your local museums or performing arts groups to have free or reduced-fee programs for children. "Arts Cards," which parents can purchase each year, offer real deals for youngsters on performances and museums. Start such a program in your community (see Resources).

Support children's museums or start your own. Children's museums are exciting environments that allow children to discover the arts for themselves. San Francisco's Exploratorium, an internationally renowned museum of art and science, is one model for hands-on, interactive learning activities that are as engaging as a video arcade (see Resources).

Make a donation to a toy library. The United States has over 400 toy libraries lodged in public libraries, schools, and hospitals, where children can check out toys to play with at home. Toy libraries also provide children with disabilities with quality, specially adapted toys, help child-care providers supplement their play, and help parents become better consumers of toys. Write to the USA Toy Library Association to identify your local library (see Resources).

If you are an artist, consider working with kids. Professional artists and children are a winning combination. Their unique viewpoint can be a significant contribution to your own perceptions, as well as a poignant voice for their own advocacy.

Precita Eyes Mural Arts Center is the brain-child of mother and artist Susan Cervantes. Her teenage son's interest in graffiti art inspired her efforts to create public space and appreciation for this cross-cultural mural movement. Through her efforts child muralists have decorated many schools and recreation centers in San Francisco.

Documentary photographer Jim Hubbard formed the Shooting Back Education and Media Center in Washington, D.C. While producing a documentary on homeless and disadvantaged children, he discovered that his "subjects" had a fascination and talent for photography and a unique perspective on their own lives. Intrigued, he handed over his cameras to the children and let them take their own pictures. Buoyed by their sense of wonder and ebullience despite their hard lives, his Media Center created a national traveling photography show called "Shooting Back—a Photographic View of Life by Homeless Children." He organizes a local "Shooting Back" movement everywhere the show travels.

An unusual alliance between San Francisco artist Ruth Asawa, the school district, and a local recycling program helped revive a program to recycle industrial and home scraps (paper, cloth, rubber, wire, and all manner of creative trash) to use for children's art projects. With vacant space, a few classrooms, and a small gymnasium provided by the schools, SCRAP is providing a treasure-trove of creative materials to schools, social services, and non-profit community organizations.

Remember that the richness of life is found in slower moments, that the formation of creative young minds is accomplished not only by the hours spent in the classroom but also by watching tree branches move and the dust fall, and the love within families flourishes when there is time for love.

—Richard Louv, *Childhood's Future*

Resources

Organizations

Exploratorium
3601 Lyon Street
San Francisco, CA 94123
(800) 359–9899
Find out about this innovative,
nationally recognized learning
museum. Ask for a mail order
catalogue for gifts and learning tools
that foster creativity.

USA Toy Library Association
2530 Crawford Avenue, Suite 111
Evanston, IL 60201
(708) 864–3330

Young Audiences
115 E. 92nd Street
New York, NY 10128-1603
(212) 831–8110
This advocacy and information
clearinghouse promotes quality arts
education for children. Ask for
information on developing Arts Cards
in your community.

Publications

The National Endowment for the
Arts, in collaboration with national
education organizations and
Hallmark Foundation, have
produced a series of five brochures
to help children develop artistic
skills in the home, community,
and schools. The brochures are
available for 50 cents a set from:

Consumer Information Center-2C
P.O. Box 100
Pueblo, CO 81009
(719) 948–3334

Chapter 11

Feed a Hungry Child

My picture's about a kid. When he came home
from school, he didn't see lunch on the table. So
he waited for dinner, but there wasn't any dinner.
They ran out of food . . . and he's kinda sad.

—Fourth-grader describing the picture he had
just drawn

Know the Facts

If there are poor children in your community, there are hungry
children.

- **Over 5.5 million children in the United States don't have
  enough food to eat**—that's one in eight.
- **Another 6 million kids are at risk of going hungry:** Once many
  families pay rent and bills, little or nothing is left for food. If
  they get food stamps, these only last a week or two. When this
  happens babies drink sugar-water or watered-down formula, children go to bed hungry or get by on crackers or noodles, or the
  families will eat at the local soup kitchen.

**Hunger is devastating to children, and haunts them all through
their lives.**

- Pregnant women who don't get enough food have smaller and
  sicker babies.
- Inadequate nutrition during childhood stunts growth and brain
  development, increases susceptibility to infections, and impedes
  learning.

The social and psychological impact of being a hungry kid in an
abundant and affluent country is no less devastating: shame, fear, family disintegration, school absenteeism, and violence are often the results. Think of how difficult and unhappy your or your friends' kids are
when they are hungry once in a while. It's no wonder poor kids get depressed, alienated, and desperate.

We can prevent hunger. Programs exist that could ensure that *every* poor child in America gets enough nutritious food to eat. But some are not fully funded, and others are not effectively administered. Private programs, such as food pantries and soup kitchens, cannot begin to solve the problem.

- Food stamps, the major food program in America, fail to reach over half of the children whose families qualify.
- The U.S. Conference of Mayors reports that in 80% of cities, emergency food programs routinely turn away hungry people due to lack of resources.

What You Can Do to End Hunger . . .

. . . At Home

Volunteer your time.   Find out what your local food programs need, and lend your time and skills. Whether it's cooking, counseling, serving, sorting, driving, weeding, fund raising, board work, or special expertise, a good program will find a niche for you.

Donate food.   Your local soup kitchen, food pantry, gleaning program, or county food bank always needs more food and money to serve hungry kids and their families. Participate in church or community food drives or fund-raising campaigns year-round, not just during the holidays!

Grow food for hungry kids.   If you have a garden, dedicate a part of your plot to a soup kitchen. Salad greens and vegetables add interest and nutrition to menus.

Your catered affairs can also feed the hungry. Vow never to cater a party (at home or at work) without making a plan ahead of time to donate the leftovers to your local food or homeless program.

. . . In Your Community

Check out your local supermarket.   Many supermarket chains now encourage shoppers to purchase donation slips that go to Food For All, a national charitable organization. Encourage your supermarket to participate, or to set up a food bin, or to donate change to food programs (see Resources).

Urge restaurants to donate extra food. Ask local restaurants to give leftover food (there are large amounts every day) to the hungry. One Berkeley, California, resident started a program, called Daily Bread, out of her home. Using her telephone and a box of index cards, she coordinates hundreds of volunteers who pick up tons of extra food every month—from bakeries, restaurants, and grocery stores—and deliver it to soup kitchens and food pantries. Today hundreds of organizations operate programs across the country that prevent needless waste and feed the hungry.

Join the Public Debate: Prevent Hunger in America

Get involved in community hunger prevention. If you already support charitable feeding efforts, consider going one step further. Start your own grass-roots "hunger-free zone" project. Work to make freedom from hunger a basic right for all American children. **If every volunteer and donor to local charitable feeding programs also took action for permanent solutions, we would end hunger in America.**

Get plugged into the network. A state and national antihunger movement has been growing since the mid-1970s. Call the Food Research and Action Center, and find out who's who in your state and local community. It's easy to become a community food activist. Through your local or state group, you can help champion state and federal legislation that improves child nutrition programs, or you can protect programs from yearly budget cut attempts or participate in education and action campaigns.

Nutrition programs are well-documented savers of money, health, and lives. For every dollar spent to feed pregnant mothers, we save $4 because their babies are born bigger and healthier. Participation in school feeding programs improves children's attendance and test scores. If we don't pay now with a little time, energy and money, we'll pay much more later—and children and our society will needlessly suffer in the process.

Follow the four-step F.O.O.D. process—Find, Organize, Outreach, Develop. With your local antihunger coalition, your friends, or a community or church group you belong to, you can:

1. **Find the Food Gaps.** Conduct a "community food diagnosis" to find out what programs exist, how many children are unserved, and what access barrier needs to come down. Ask questions:
   - Does your food bank or pantry provide nutrition education?
   - Are local restaurants or farms throwing away perfectly good food?
   - Does the local WIC program (Supplemental Food Program for Women, Infants, and Children) serve children, or can it only afford to serve women and infants?
   - Do all schools in your area participate in the School Breakfast program?
   - Do all homeless families at your local shelter know they may be eligible for emergency food stamps?
   - Is the City Parks and Recreation Department running the federally funded Summer Food Service program this year? (The food coalition in your state, or the Food Research and Action Center, can help you learn what programs your community's children are entitled to.)

2. **Organize to get them filled.** Get on the agenda at city council and school board meetings, write letters, call the media, and generally raise hell! Keep at it: Everyone agrees that children should not be hungry.

3. **Outreach to Hungry Kids.** Distribute fliers at schools and supermarkets, get radio spots going, or help set up a food referral sys-

tem. Many families are confused about or unaware of available food programs.

4. **Develop Community Support.** Let members of your community know about various food programs, and enlist their support.

Kids helping kids. Children understand hunger and are motivated to do something to help other children. Order *Kids Ending Hunger: What Can We Do?* for hundreds of ideas (see Resources). A child who is a hunger activist now will be one for life.

Remember: One in ten Americans is now getting food stamps—and half of them are kids!

Resources

Organizations

Bread for the World
802 Rhode Island Avenue, N.E.
Washington, D.C. 20018
(202) 269–0200
This Christian membership organization for churches and individuals advocates antihunger policies.

Food Industry Crusade Against
    Hunger
800 Connecticut Avenue, N.W.
Washington, D.C. 20006
(202) 429–4555
This group raises money for local, national, and international hunger programs; coordinates supermarkets nationwide to support hunger programs. Ask how your supermarket can participate.

Food Research and Action Center
1875 Connecticut Avenue, N.W.,
    Suite 540
Washington, D.C. 20009
(202) 986–2200

This group coordinates federal legislative activities and a national antihunger network; publishes reports, newsletters, and organizing manuals on federal food-assistance programs.

Second Harvest National
    Food Bank Network
116 South Michigan Avenue, Suite 4
Chicago, IL 60603
(312) 263–2303
This is the headquarters and clearinghouse for most of the food banks in the country. Call to find out about the food bank nearest you.

Publications

Kids Ending Hunger: What Can We Do? A Get-into-Action Book for Kids and Their Parents and Teachers, by John Rosemond. Kansas City: Andrews & McMeel, 1992. This book has many exciting ideas about what kids themselves can do. To order, call (800) 826–4216.

Chapter 12

Hire a Youth

America may have the worst school-to-work
transition system of any advanced industrialized
country. Students who know few adults to help
them get their first job are left to sink or swim.

—Commission on the Skills of the Work Force

While a small fraction of America has the
conceptual skills to participate in this new world
economy, most Americans do not. The only way to reverse this trend is
to invest in the future productive capacities of Americans. But the U.S.
has been doing exactly the opposite.

—Robert B. Reich, Secretary of Labor

Know the Facts

Every month an average of 1.1 million teenagers and 1.2 million young
adults are looking for work. Remember when you were 16 and you
wanted to be treated like a grown-up? You just needed to have someone take a chance on you.

A child's first job is one of the most important steps in preparing to
become self-sufficient. But it's getting harder all the time for young
people to get employment. Employers tend to greet kids with a mix-
ture of distrust, disrespect, and low expectations. The kids don't get
the experience, and companies don't get the benefit of the special talents young people bring to the workplace: enthusiasm, stamina, openness, and hope.

What You Can Do . . .

. . . At Home

Teach good attitudes toward work. Kids who are expected to do
jobs at home develop more self-esteem than kids whose parents do all
the work for them. Unfortunately, for most kids (and most adults) the
word "chores" implies a burden, not a duty. Develop a system in which

children and adults share work. This helps children understand their role in maintaining the welfare of the family, and keeps them from feeling put upon when asked to work.

Don't forget those one-shot jobs. When you have a particularly big job at home, like repainting or hauling, spare your own back and hire some young people (or your own kids) at a reasonable hourly wage. Many community agencies maintain listings of kids who are interested in temporary jobs. Call your United Way or local high school to find the agencies in your community.

. . . In Your Community

Encourage business to hire youth. If young people work at your favorite store, tell the manager that you think it's great. If not, suggest calling a local youth employment agency or the local Private Industry Council for information on putting kids to work (see Resources). Encourage large companies too. Ask the members of your Chamber of Commerce if they have made hiring youth a priority. Inquire at a major industry in your community whether they have a policy of hiring youth. Big businesses sometimes give money to agencies that train young people, but they rarely hire them. Let businesses know that hiring youth is the only way they'll ever really know how well their training money is spent.

Have a vacancy? Hire a youth! If you are an employer and have never hired a young person, think about it. If you have concerns, you're not alone. Fortunately, many community agencies will help you restructure jobs to make them fit into a young person's after-school or weekend schedule; they'll even meet with your other employees to prepare them to have a young person working at their side. You'll also find substantial tax benefits for providing this kind of support for young people. You pay a worker, who is backed up by a supporting agency, and you get a tax deduction for doing it!

Here are some tips on how to make employing a youth an enriching experience for everyone:

- **Be patient and positive.** Be understanding and helpful, but do not lower your standards. Let kids know when they're messing up. This gives the youth the option of learning to behave like an adult.

"Don't you think he'd make a great assistant?!"

- **Enjoy yourself.** Young workers are a lot of fun. They have fresh views and new ideas. Listen!
- **Remember your own early experiences.** Remember your first job? The sudden realization that your socks didn't match, how scary the receptionist was, or how old the boss was, the adults who took a special interest in you and showed you the ropes—these memories can help you empathize with your employee instead of becoming an adversary.

Become a mentor. Kids need role models, and adults need the satisfaction of sharing their experience. Many community organizations can match you with a youth who needs your help. Start with your United Way, or the high school counseling department.

- **Job shadowing** is an easy way to show a young person what the world of work is like. A young person accompanies you on your daily routine.
- **Take a youth to lunch.** Talk about what you do at work, and be open to questions. You'd be surprised at how often an informal

meeting like this helps reduce a young person's anxiety when he or she confronts a real interview.

- **Talk to a class or youth group about your profession.** Many kids have no idea what types of career options are open to them. Hearing about specific jobs they might strive for is important. It is especially important for young people to see role models of different races, and for young girls to see successful women. Call the local high school principal or youth organization to offer your services.

Join the Public Debate: Support Job-Training Programs

Lobby the schools. Check out the vocational and job-readiness programs in your school district. Write a letter to your local school board and let them know that you believe we owe it to our future to provide quality training in contemporary job skills. Many school districts have shut down their vocational-training programs, hurting young people who don't plan or can't afford to go to college.

Support federally funded youth employment programs. The federal government has played a major role in providing the youth of America with early employment opportunities, but in the 1980s the youth jobs programs were drastically cut. Rally behind President Clinton's national service and youth opportunity proposals and other federal jobs programs for youth.

Don't let youth employees be exploited—blow the whistle. Child labor abuses are a growing national concern. Many experts believe that exploitive employers can interfere with the school and health of their young labor force. Work is great, but moderation and safety are essential. For example, children under age 14 can't work, children under 16 can't work during school hours or after 7 P.M. on weeknights. All children must have "working papers," and no child can hold a hazardous job.

Most people don't realize that there are virtually no routine investigations of potential child labor abuses. Action is taken by the state and federal government only when a complaint is made. It is up to you. If your child gets a job, make sure the law is obeyed. To get a citizen guide to child labor standards or to report possible abuses in your community, contact the U.S. Department of Labor office in your city, or your state's human resources office.

Remember: Kids are either tomorrow's work force or tomorrow's social problems. We must prepare *all* our children.

Resources

Organizations

National Child Labor
   Committee
1501 Broadway, Suite 1111
New York, NY 10036
(212) 840–1801
Ask for information on child labor violations and other workplace issues related to children.

National Youth Employment
   Coalition
1501 Broadway, Suite 1111
New York, NY 10036
(212) 840–1801
Ask for information on youth employment issues, and how you can start a community coalition that fosters greater youth employment.

KIDS ARE OUR BUSINESS

Chapter 13

Make Your Company Child-Friendly

Companies are sounding the alarm. Telephone sales jobs are going begging in Boston because MCI cannot find qualified workers; textile workers are no longer able to operate their computerized machines; and aircraft manufacturers in California have teamed up out of necessity to train employees. Companies such as New York telephone report hiring frustrations of epic proportions—57,000 applicants have to be tested to find 2,100 who are qualified to fill entry-level technical jobs.

—Commission on the Skills of the American Work Force

Know the Facts

Corporations across America are facing the unpleasant reality that without their leadership and support, today's first-graders won't make it to college. They may not even make it through junior high school. And they will not be able to join the work force of tomorrow, when for the first time the majority of jobs will require postsecondary education. In response, more and more businesses today have made a commitment to children. In fact, there are school-business partnerships in almost 40% of the nation's schools. Here are some of the things business can do:

- Businesses "adopt" schools, giving needed money, materials, and expertise.
- Companies provide child-care benefits to employees.
- Corporate executives act as mentors to youngsters, or "principals for a day" in urban schools.
- Businesses offer training internships for students.
- Business leaders participate in school reform projects.
- Corporate foundations fund model children's services.

Business can be a powerful ally for America's children.

What You Can Do to Make
Your Company Child-Friendly . . .

Very often it is the employees rather than management that promotes commitment to children in the workplace. Here are some of the things you can do.

Conduct a "pro-child audit" of your company. Use the following questionnaire to determine your company's attitude toward children.

PRO-CHILD BUSINESS AUDIT

Instructions: Circle 1 for no, 2 for yes.

1. Does your company actively support education, vocational training, and other children's services in your community?   1 or 2

2. Does your company give at least 2% of pre-tax profits to the community?   1 or 2

3. Does your company lobby to support programs, such as Head Start, that help the most at-risk children in the country?   1 or 2

4. Does your company provide referrals to employees for child care and dependent child-care tax credit?   1 or 2

5. Does your company provide more than mandated disability leave for new mothers, paternity leave for new fathers, and extra employee sick days to care for sick children?   1 or 2

6. Does your company include financial support for child care in its benefits package for employees?   1 or 2

7. Does your company employ or train disadvantaged youth from your community?   1 or 2

8. Does your company provide regular information on the state of children in your community and opportunities on how employees can get involved?   1 or 2

9. Does your company provide release-time to employees who wish to volunteer in the community?   1 or 2

Now tally your score.

- 17–18: You work for a gold-star company. Give lots of credit, and try to pass on ideas to other companies.

- 13–16: Your company is above average, but read on for ideas for improvement.

- 11–12: Your company has made a decent start, but you still have lots of work to do.

- 9–10: You clearly have your work cut out for you.

If your company scored high, congratulations! If your company scored less than 17, read on.

. . . At a Large Company

Explore corporate giving.

- **Talk to the corporate giving officer.** Ask if your company makes charitable donations to children's causes.
- **Make specific recommendations.** Encourage donations to children's organizations. Share information on specific organizations that you think merit support. Corporations are much more likely to give money to organizations that employees recommend. Encourage your company to create a policy of matching gifts made by employees.
- **Calculate what percentage of pre-tax profits of the company go to charitable donations.** Encourage your company to increase its

percentage. All companies should give a minimum of 2%. A few gold star companies like Mervyn's, a discount department store chain, donate 5% of their profits to community services.

- **Suggest specific in-kind services your company might offer.** Gifts in Kind America, a national organization founded by United Way, annually distributes millions of dollars worth of materials that have been donated by American businesses—clothes, building supplies, household goods, personal-hygiene products, office equipment (see Resources).

Hint: If you are promoting the idea of community involvement to supervisors or managers, clip positive press stories about other companies doing good—preferably a competitor. Look for stories that cite the benefits of child-friendly policies (reduced absenteeism, employee loyalty, higher productivity, and lower turnover); or stories about collaboratives your company could join.

Make child care an issue.   Form a child-care lunch caucus. Meet with employees of your company who are raising young children. Evaluate your company's child-care policies and make recommendations for improvements. Look at such issues as parental leave, making child care a benefit like health care, flex-time, time off for teacher conferences, providing employees with childcare information, or setting up a child-care center on-site.

Look into youth job training.   Form a youth-training task force to determine which job-training programs your company can best offer: for example, internships, summer jobs, or "shadowing" programs (see chapter 12). Bring in community leaders to address your group on the possibilities, then sell the idea to your managers. Identify specific jobs that could be done by youth, and figure out what it would take to employ at-risk youth.

Don't forget to volunteer.   Contact agencies that serve children and youth in your community, make a list of volunteer opportunities available, and get the list into your company's publications on a regular basis. Devise a workable system that would allow employees to use release time for volunteering.

Oppose company positions you find objectionable. In California a number of major corporations offered support for a ballot measure calling for draconian cuts in state child welfare spending. If your company takes a similar stand, make your voice heard. A group of employees who object may have more impact than a single voice. Your group can write a letter to the newsletter, or even to the daily newspaper. Choosing anonymity may make it "safer" for you to come out against company policy (although it will weaken the impact of the letters).

Urge your company to take a stand on pro-child issues. Counter the influence of negative corporations, like those above, by encouraging your company to be publicly pro-child. This is not only great PR for the company but a sound investment in the future work force of America. When five Fortune 500 CEOs went to Congress in 1991 to lobby for increases in federal spending for food for poor children, it made national news. They were not only promoting excellent child policy, they were changing both the image and role of corporations in America. And the clout of the business lobby won over Congress!

. . . At a Small Company

- Get a wish list from a nonprofit agency working with children, then designate the one closest to your company as a donation site.
- Offer services (desk-top publishing, advertising, catering, marketing—whatever your specialty is) pro-bono to selected nonprofits.
- Create an ongoing relationship between your business and non-profits—either assisting with fund raising, or with annual events on behalf of children and youth.
- Meet with similar businesses to explore collaboration possibilities—corporate giving, employee benefits, or other child-friendly programs.

Resources

Committee for Economic
Development
477 Madison Avenue
New York, NY 10022
(212) 688–2063
This private nonprofit research and
education organization, made up of
top business executives and presi-
dents of major universities, seeks
solutions to social problems that
affect the economy, with emphasis
on issues related to children. They
also promote child-friendly business
policies.

Gifts in Kind America
700 N. Fairfax Street, Suite 300
Alexandria, VA 22314
(703) 836–2121
This group encourages product
donations from companies and
distributes gifts to service agencies
at shipping cost. Ask how you can
participate in a gifts-in-kind
program.

Junior Achievement
1 Education Way
Colorado Springs, CO 80906
(719) 540–8000
(800) 843–6395
Affiliates in 200 cities help business
work with high school youth.

National Association of Partners
in Education
209 Madison Street, Suite 401
Alexandria, VA 22314
(703) 836–4880
This group assists businesses in
developing partnerships with schools.
Send for information packets,
newsletters, and training information.

Work and Family Institute
330 7th Avenue, 14th Floor
New York, NY 10001
(212) 465–2044
This is a clearinghouse for
information for businesses concerned
with changes in work and family
relationships. Ask for information on
parental leave and child care.

Chapter 14

Unlearn Prejudice: They're All Our Children

> I have a dream my four little children will one day live in a nation where they will not be judged by the color of their skin but by the content of their character.
>
> —Martin Luther King, Jr.

Know the Facts . . .

Never before in our history has it been more important to achieve Martin Luther King's dream. Today's children are the first truly multiracial, multicultural generation; and tensions related to race, ethnicity, and sexual identity mar the childhoods of a growing number of kids. Despite our rich diversity, we are a country steeped in prejudice. A child who is the victim of prejudice experiences not only emotional pain and social and economic barriers, but also permanent damage to his or her confidence and sense of self-worth.

Children are not born biased, but they do begin to notice differences at a very young age. By age five, children begin to absorb society's prejudicial messages and fears. Between ages seven and nine, children's awareness of differences may be transformed into full-blown prejudice.

Our unconscious attitudes and beliefs lead us to view the world in strange ways. For example, is there really something that can be called "flesh color"? Can we really use the term "minorities," meaning "nonwhite," to describe the majority of the world's people? It is imperative that our children unlearn prejudice—and develop a true appreciation for each other. It is also imperative that adults, who are responsible for molding society, unlearn the prejudice that allows us to assign a growing number of our children to second-class lives.

. . . About Children of Color

People automatically think you're a gang member, just because you're walking down the street with other kids. I went to a store. The store manager chased us out because of our race.

—14-year-old Hispanic male

By the year 2000, 42% of all public school students in the United States will be children of color. By the middle of the next century, the majority of all our children will be nonwhite. In some states, like California, this is already the case.

The sad reality is that children of color are far less likely to experience the benefits of our society than white children: They receive poorer medical care than white children, their teachers often assume they will fail, and they often anticipate an adult life of unemployment and closed doors. Today, the gap between white children and nonwhite children is getting larger, rather than smaller:

- The poverty rate for African-American children is three times that of white children.
- Hispanic children are twice as likely to be without health insurance as white children.
- African-American and Hispanic youth are suspended from school at a rate three times that of their white counterparts.

- Only half of Hispanic students graduate from high school, compared to three-quarters of white students.
- African-American babies are more than twice as likely as white babies to be born underweight.
- The median income of Hispanic families with children is 60% that of white families with children.
- Forty percent of African-American teens looking for a job can't find one—more than double the rate for white teens.

. . . About Immigrant and Refugee Children

I remember teaching a geography spelling lesson to mostly Cambodian youngsters and using a "hangman" lesson for spelling . . . and having this youngster say to me, "You know, that's how my parents died." That was my coming of age as a teacher.

—Teacher, Newcomer High School, San Francisco, from
Crossing the Schoolhouse Border, by California Tomorrow

We are a nation of immigrants, and that has never been more true than it is today:

- At least 2.7 million school-aged immigrants now live in the United States.
- As many as 100 different languages or dialects are spoken in some large, urban school districts in U.S. cities.

Many have come here to escape war, poverty, and political repression. They have lived in situations most Americans cannot even imagine: Some have lived in refugee camps for years, others have left behind family members, others may have no family at all.

The children of refugees have some problems in common: learning a new language, adjusting to a new culture, dealing with racism, harassment, and hostility. Their families cannot help them with these problems. Indeed, roles are often reversed—they have to help their parents by talking to the landlord, arranging for medical care, and getting legal help. Sometimes these children have to take care of siblings or work to help out their families, and are unable to do their schoolwork.

Some have lost family members in war; some have severe emotional problems; some feel very isolated, caught between the culture they left behind and their new home. Many of these children have had no one to talk to about their lives. In the book *Crossing the Schoolhouse Border,* one tenth-grade Chinese girl says, "I don't know who I am. Am I the good Chinese daughter? Am I an American teenager? . . . I never feel really comfortable with myself."

. . . About Gay and Lesbian Youth

I knew I was different from the time I was 12 years old. At first I didn't understand it. And when I did, I couldn't talk to anyone—not my friends, not my family. I tried to fit in, to go to dances, to laugh at gay jokes. But I couldn't. Finally, when I was 17, I left home. I didn't want to hurt my family.

—Young gay man recalling his childhood

Gay men and lesbians do not "choose" a "lifestyle." Just like heterosexuals, they share a sexual orientation that is most likely biologically determined in the womb. They constitute a consistent 10% of every segment of the population. Unfortunately, young people who happen to be gay are frequently singled out simply for being themselves.

Most children who are ridiculed can run to their parents or peers for comfort. Gay and lesbian youth, however, rarely can. Fearing more ridicule or rejection, they hide their personal needs from parents and friends. Society's norms deprive them of the chance even to tentatively explore their sexuality during their junior high or high school years. They live in a world of secrets, knowing that revealing their feelings makes them vulnerable to violence and scorn: They are mainstream exiles, and many are social casualties.

- Gay and lesbian young people account for a full third of teen suicides annually. They have a high rate of drug and alcohol dependence, and many suffer physical abuse at the hands of parents and peers.
- Statistics from a center for runaway street youth in San Francisco show that more than 90% of young people who identify themselves as gay or lesbian have been sexually, physically, and psychologically abused. Many are forced to leave home because their parents cannot accept them for themselves.

All young people need role models. Unfortunately, the gay people portrayed on TV and in movies almost always fit trivial cultural stereotypes, or are negatively cast as murderers and criminals. Prejudices that are no longer acceptable for any other group are still invoked against this population.

Remember: All young people who are just becoming aware of their sexuality need personal support. Gay and lesbian youth are no exception.

What You Can Do . . .

. . . To Model Openness and Cultural Sensitivity

Own up to your biases and educate yourself.   Like it or not, everyone has prejudices. Try to figure out your own. Do you instinctively stiffen up when you sit next to a person of a different ethnic group? Do you assume that a person who speaks with an accent doesn't understand complex issues? Do you automatically dismiss the idea that a young person may be gay? We can't help our children overcome their biases unless we come to terms with our own.

Let a child see you stand up for yourself.   Inaction in the face of abusive behavior or derogatory comments often means acceptance. All children benefit from the example of a strong, self-assured adult who refuses to accept abusive behavior. If you do nothing more than say that you disagree, it will be enough. One woman remembers, "One of the most enduring memories of my childhood was seeing my mother tell a cab driver who was dropping us off at our house, how offended she was by his anti-Semitic remarks. I had never seen her so passionate. I was very young, but I remember being so proud."

Talk to a child about the variety of human experience.   Don't encourage your children to be "color-blind"—to pretend race doesn't exist. Instead, aim to increase their awareness and appreciation of differences and similarities among people. For example, all people eat food, but each cultural group has its own special way of preparing food. Just as we can enjoy Mexican, Chinese, and Thai food, we can appreciate that there are special qualities to every kind of people.

Always show respect.   Don't laugh at jokes that ridicule people because of their differences. For example, jokes about gay people are commonplace, and even the most enlightened tend to think laughing is okay. Each time children see discrimination supported with conspiratorial laughter, they see cruelty rewarded.

Get involved.   Step in when you see a young person being intolerant of another because of differences. Take the time to talk with the young person so that he or she will understand why you disapprove. Support the child who has been hurt. If possible, meet with the parents and arrange a time when the children can come together and talk about their problem.

. . . To Expose Children to Diversity

Choose diversity in playthings.   Provide books, dolls, toys, wall decorations, and music that reflect diverse images and lifestyles that children may not see elsewhere—for your own children, and for the materials you donate to children's programs.

Attend multicultural events.   Visit museums, see films, attend multicultural celebrations, celebrate holidays . . . go out of your way to find places for your child, or children you know, to learn about other cultures and diverse heritages. Support these activities with your volunteer time or financial backing.

Seek out integrated situations for your family.   Many children live and go to school with children who look just like them. Whether it be your neighborhood, your child's school, after-school activities, summer camps—try to find a program that includes all types of children. Let other children help broaden your child's horizons.

. . . To Make Your School and Community Bias-Free

Review the materials your child gets in school.   Make sure books and handouts from school have fair, multicultural representation. As one Hispanic college student says, "It wasn't 'til I got to college that I even knew you could study anything besides white people." Let the school know that it bothers you if the materials do not reflect diversity. If the school has very little material on other cultures, or on issues related to sexual identity, consider donating a book or two to the school library. Encourage your school to establish an ethnic studies curriculum.

Arrange speakers and presentations for your school. Encourage parents born in other countries to speak to the class. Children have all kinds of questions about differences. They are generally unprepared for life in an increasingly multicultural society. Organize an activity involving ethnic food or music that brings kids together on an informal basis.

Protest stereotyping. Call a TV station when you see children's shows that promote stereotypes. Urge your local toy store manager to purchase toys such as dolls, books, and puzzles that reflect diversity. Ask your local card store to sell greeting cards that show multicultural children.

Report hate crimes. Don't walk away. Stopping hate crimes is everyone's responsibility. Call the U.S. Department of Justice to report: (800) 347–HATE.

Help children protest injustice. Take children to a rally or a protest. Encourage them to initiate their own actions at school. They can write letters, plan rallies, initiate mediations, circulate petitions.

Join the Public Debate: Work for Equal Opportunity

Support policies and programs that advocate equal opportunity for all children. Oppose policies that discriminate. Fight to preserve and expand civil rights—in your local community, your state, and in the nation.

He drew a circle that shut me out—
Heretic, rebel, a thing to flout
But love and I had the wit to win:
We drew a circle that took him in.

—Edward Markham

Resources

Note: There are many types of prejudice discussed throughout this book. Several chapters address the special needs of girls. Chapter 9 is on children with disabilities, and chapter 24 discusses children with AIDS.

Organizations

Anti-Defamation League
823 U.N. Plaza
New York, NY 10017
(212) 490–2525
Ask for a free information packet. The ADL has produced "A World of Difference," a nationally acclaimed prejudice reduction program.

Aspira Association
1112 16th Street, N.W., Suite 340
Washington, D.C. 20036
(202) 835–3600
Advocacy for Hispanic youth. Works with network of 2,000 community organizations.

Federation of Parents and Friends of Lesbians and Gays
1012 14th Street., N.W.
Washington, D.C. 20005
(202) 638–4200
(800) 4–FAMILY
Ask for information on homosexuality and on support groups for parents and friends of gay children. They have 300 local affiliates (call the 800 number to find the chapter nearest you).

National Coalition of Advocates for Students
100 Boylston Street, Suite 737
Boston, MA 02216
(617) 357–8507
Ask for information on immigrant students, and how to improve schools for all students.

Southern Poverty Law Center
Teaching Tolerance Program
400 Washington Avenue
Montgomery, AL 36104
(205) 264–0286
This group promotes interracial and intercultural understanding in the classroom. Ask for teaching kits, videotapes, teacher guides, magazine.

Publications

Common Bonds: Anti-Bias Teaching in a Diverse Society, by Deborah A. Byrnes and Gary Kiger. Wheaton, MD: Association for Childhood Education International, 1992. To order, call (800) 423–3563 ($15.00).

Crossing the Schoolhouse Border: Immigrant Students and the California Public Schools, by Laurie Olsen. San Francisco, CA: California Tomorrow, 1988. To order, call (415) 441–7631.

Cultural Backgrounds and Educational Issues: A Guide on Asian and Pacific Islander American Students, by John Nobuia Tshuchida. Washington, D.C.: National Education Association, 1991. To order, call (202) 822–7220.

Kids Explore America's African American Heritage (1993), and *Kids Explore America's Hispanic Heritage* (1992), by Westridge Young Writers Workshop. Santa Fe, NM: John Muir Publishing. Written for kids by 85 elementary school children in Littleton, Colorado, under the inspirational direction of teacher Judy Cozzens. Excellent, and beautifully produced. To order, call (800) 888–7504.

Kids With Courage: True Stories About Young People Making a Difference, by Barbara A. Lewis. Minneapolis: Free Spirit Publishing, 1991. To order, call (800) 735–7323 ($14.95).

Positively Different: Creating a Bias Free Environment for Young Children, by Anna Consuelo Matiella. Santa Cruz, CA: Network Publication, 1992. Resource handbook for parents and teachers. To order, call the ETR Association at (800) 321–4407 ($14.95).

Some Do Care: Contemporary Lives of Moral Commitment, by Anne Colby and William Damon. New York: Macmillan, 1992.

Tools for Empowering Young Children, by Louise Derman-Sparts and the Anti-Bias Curriculum Task Force. Book for parents and teachers to help children understand bias and analyze children's books for racism and other bias. You can order this curriculum as well as anti-bias posters for children from the National Association for the Education of Young Children, by calling (800) 424–2460.

Chapter 15

Stop Cigarette Ads from Killing Our Kids

Joe Camel is cool. He has his own philosophies. When Joe throws a party, only smooth characters need apply. He has his own partying place. He's definitely a stud.

—Comments from 16-year-old kids who started smoking at age 12, from *Parents Press*, Berkeley, California

Know the Facts

Tobacco kills more Americans each year than alcohol, cocaine, crack, heroin, homicides, suicides, car accidents, fires, and AIDS *combined*.

- Every day the tobacco industry addicts more than 3,000 kids to nicotine, a drug at least as addictive as heroin.
- Tobacco is the leading drug problem in America today. Every year the tobacco industry kills 434,000 smokers, and the air pollution from secondhand tobacco smoke kills another 53,000 non-smokers.

Spend one minute reading the following briefing—it tells you all you need to know to become an antismoking crusader.

ONE-MINUTE BRIEFING ON TOBACCO AND KIDS

Tobacco is immensely profitable. It costs less than a penny to manufacture a cigarette, and a package of cigarettes sells for a couple of dollars. As a result tobacco industry profits exceeded $7.2 billion in 1989. Unfortunately for this highly profitable industry, it kills off 1,200 of its customers a day, and another 3,500 succeed in stopping smoking. To replace these smokers, the tobacco industry must recruit new smokers—**and those new smokers are children.**

Tobacco is the most advertised product in America. This advertising, based on cowboys and cartoon camels, sports and glamorous models, reaches children effectively. Half of all smokers are addicted by age 13, and virtually all start by 18. These children rarely appreciate the dangers of smoking or how addictive nicotine is.

- Philip Morris's Marlboro is the leading children's cigarette; about two-thirds of the children's market.
- Thanks to its "Smooth Joe" cartoon camel campaign, RJ Reynolds's Camel cigarettes are rapidly growing in popularity among children. Joe Camel is as familiar among six year olds as Mickey Mouse.
- The tobacco industry spends millions of dollars on political campaign contributions and lobbying to prevent the government from imposing meaningful restrictions on tobacco promotions to children.

In addition to causing heart disease, strokes, cancer, and a variety of other diseases in adult smokers, breathing the air pollution caused by smoking—so-called passive smoking—is a major danger for children. In 1993 the U.S. Environmental Protection Agency recognized secondhand tobacco smoke as a Group A carcinogen, the most dangerous category—together with such toxins as vinyl chloride, arsenic, and asbestos—and concluded that secondhand smoke was particularly dangerous for children. It causes pneumonia, bronchitis, and asthma. Smoking is also particularly toxic to the developing fetus.

Thanks to its political power, few government programs are directed at effective control of the tobacco industry. It is up to individual parents and citizen groups to protect children from the industry.

What You Can Do to Stop Smoking . . .

. . . At Home

Share the facts about smoking. Share the one-minute briefing you just read with others. Copy or tear out the page and carry it with you if you need help remembering the information.

Always request the smoke-free section in restaurants. Most restaurants around the country are required to have a nonsmoking section. Many restaurants are already smoke-free.

Encourage kids to be militant nonsmokers. When someone tries to smoke around them, encourage kids to politely but firmly request that the person stop or smoke somewhere else. Tell them clearly that smoking makes you sick, and that it's stupid to kill yourself by getting hooked on cigarettes.

Teach your kids to be skeptics. Teach your kids to distrust tobacco advertising. Show that smoking is not cool, that the cigarette-selling job is totally fake—a con job.

Help your child stop smoking. If your child has started to smoke, work with him or her to stop as soon as possible. The younger someone starts smoking and the longer they smoke, the more damage is done and the harder it is to stop later in life. Be sure to praise your child for having the courage and perseverance it takes to break an addiction that is said to be more difficult to kick than heroin!

If you smoke, stop! You'll live longer to be a good parent and grandparent; and you'll stop harming your children and those around you.

If you are pregnant, don't smoke! Unborn babies and cigarettes don't mix. Smoking leads to low-birthweight babies and other problems in newborns. If you are pregnant, quit smoking now. If your wife is pregnant, do not smoke or permit anyone else to smoke around her.

. . . In Your Community

Make your workplace smoke free.   If you own your own business, you can do this yourself. If you are an employee, join with other employees to urge management toward this goal. Encourage businesses you patronize to become smoke free and post signs to that effect.

Protest tobacco industry promotional events.   The tobacco industry spends millions on sponsoring events to sell cigarettes or other tobacco. There are even instances of hospitals serving as local sponsors for the Virginia Slims Tennis Tournament! Join with your children to protest these events, and pressure local organizations to refuse to participate in them.

Urge publications you read to refuse tobacco advertising.   If they don't carry cigarette advertising, they cannot be blackmailed into silence on issues related to tobacco.

Join the Public Debate: Fight for Smoke-Free Living

A small group of committed citizens can do many things at the local level to protect children from the tobacco industry. You will be most effective when you join with other people and organizations in working for political change. Start with local nonsmokers' rights activist groups, such as Americans for Nonsmokers' Rights or various chapters of GASP (Group Against Smoke Pollution), the American Cancer Society, the American Lung Association, or the American Heart Association.

At the Local Level

Most meaningful tobacco control has taken place at the local level. A few motivated, well-organized individuals can accomplish amazing victories despite the tobacco industry's massive resources.

- Work for local legislation requiring smoke-free public places, workplaces, and restaurants.
- Eliminate tobacco advertising and promotion from public property.
- Eliminate all tobacco vending machines, an important source of tobacco for children.

I was a little nervous the first time I went into a bar because the vending machine was in the center of the room. I walked directly to the machine, which was in plain view of the bartender who was watching me, and purchased cigarettes from the machine. Every time, no one stopped me or tried to talk to me. The only comment was one man saying to the man next to him, "She's not a regular, she doesn't have holes in her coat."

—Christine, age 12, from *Kids Say Don't Smoke*

At the State and Federal Level

- Support increases in the tax on tobacco. High prices are an effective deterrent to smoking by children. The resulting revenues can go to important underfunded services to children.
- Support strong regulation of the tobacco industry.

The Prime Minister of Norway has committed to making the country smoke-free by the year 2000! Certainly, we can at least curtail advertising and access to children.

Resources

Organizations

Americans for Nonsmokers' Rights
2530 San Pablo Avenue, Suite J
Berkeley, CA 94702
(510) 841–3032
This is a national advocate group for nonsmokers with information on how to promote smoke-free ordinances. Ask about their educational program for students to encourage their peers not to smoke.

Smoke-Free Education Services
375 South End Avenue, Suite 32-F
New York, NY 10280
(212) 912–0960
This public education campaign sponsors the Smoke-Free America ad contest.

Stop Teenage Addiction to Tobacco (STAT)
121 Lyman Street, Suite 210
Springfield, MA 01103
(800) 998–7828
This advocacy and public education group opposes tobacco advertising and vending machines; ask for their newsletter and for reports on youth and smoking.

Publications

Kids Say Don't Smoke, by Andrew Tobias. New York: Workman Publishing, 1990. Contains posters for the New York City smoke-free ad contest; a moving testimonial about why kids shouldn't smoke.

Chapter 16

Just Say No to the Liquor Lobby

A billion bottles of beer on the wall, a billion bottles of beer . . .

Know the Facts

That's right—**American kids consume over a billion bottles of beer each year!** Drinking by high school kids rarely even raises the eyebrows of most parents and other adults. "It's part of growing up," we say. "And compared to other drugs, it's harmless." Well, think again.

- Alcohol is the leading cause of death among teenagers. Over 3,000 kids die in car crashes related to alcohol each year. It is the number one teenage drug problem, and it doesn't stop there: Most alcoholics start drinking in their teenage years.
- Of the 21 million students attending grades seven through 12 nationwide, over 10 million drink.

The alcohol industry targets our kids. The liquor industry spends over $2 billion a year "educating" teenagers and other potential consumers.

- Between the ages of two and 18, American children see 100,000 television commercials for beer. Many of these ads specifically target youth with themes of rebellion, masculinity, success, risk-taking, fun, and sex.
- The association between alcohol and professional sports has become so familiar that most of us don't even question the absurdity of liquor industry ads displayed on high-speed sports cars, scoreboards, and boxing rings.
- The alcohol industry promotes its products by sponsoring rock concerts and tours. The logos for the sponsoring brand appear prominently on the ads, tickets, posters, programs, and T-shirts sold in conjunction with the concerts.

Alcohol is cheap. Price is another important strategy used to target youth. Current alcohol tax policy has kept the price of alcoholic beverages low, while other beverages and consumer items have risen—even though, according to former Surgeon General C. Everett Koop, "An increase in price brought about by an increase in excise taxes prevents or delays underage youth from drinking." Nowadays, beer is often less expensive than sparkling mineral water.

What You Can Do to Stop Kids from Drinking . . .

. . . At Home

Model wise drinking habits.   You don't have to give up alcohol yourself, but you do need to examine your drinking habits to be sure you are setting a good example for kids. For example, do you drink and drive? Or do you make sure that one adult in the group is a designated driver when you go out with friends? Talk to your kids about the effects of alcohol on response time and decision-making ability.

. . . In Your Community

Work to restrict alcohol advertising.   Urge your county or city council to pass an ordinance prohibiting alcoholic beverage outdoor advertising on publicly owned property such as billboards, buses, and bus shelters. Our cities shouldn't publicly sanction the marketing of unhealthy products that contribute to social problems.

- A group of concerned citizens in San Francisco campaigned to eliminate alcohol and tobacco advertising from the city's public transportation system. The advocates centered their argument on the fact that 30,000 school children see these ads daily as they ride to and from school.
- Rev. Calvin Butts of Harlem's Abyssinian Baptist Church organized a Saturday group that whitewashes alcohol and tobacco billboards in his community. This has led to changes in ad placements by several New York alcohol and billboard companies.

Say no to events sponsored by alcohol companies.   Make your community events free of alcohol industry sponsorship. Often alcohol is a major cause of disturbances at these events. In Santa Ana, California, skeptics said that men would not attend the annual Cinco de Mayo festival if beer was not sold. But a total of 15,000 men, women, and children did show up for music, dancing, food, games, and rides—without beer.

Oppose expansion of liquor outlets in your community.   Protest the issuance of licenses to sell alcohol in communities already saturated with liquor outlets. Grounds for protest include: the character of the applicant; proximity to churches, schools, hospitals, and playgrounds; high-crime area; proximity to residences; over-concentration of licensed outlets; creation of traffic congestion problems; contrary to local zoning; and contribution to law enforcement problems.

Join the Public Debate:
Demand a *Real* War on Drugs

In 1986 the federal government launched its "war on drugs," but excluded alcohol—next to tobacco the number-one drug of choice—from the strategy. Yet the adverse public health consequences of alcohol use are the most catastrophic. Alcohol and tobacco kill perhaps *500 times* more people than cocaine, and 20 times more than all other drugs combined. Without a front on alcohol, the "war on drugs" is a phony war.

Support increases in alcohol taxes.   Support state and federal legislation to increase alcohol excise taxes, which would in turn de-

crease consumption of alcohol among youth. Increased alcohol excise taxes are also sources of revenue in tight budgetary times.

Protest beer advertising.   Become familiar with the beer codes of advertising standards, and complain about violations to the liquor companies. The standards actually prohibit much of the advertising now going on. Send copies of your complaint to the Bureau of Alcohol, Tobacco, and Firearms (see Resources). Complaints about a Coors ad in New York resulted in the ad being removed.

Support health messages on advertisements.   Advocate health messages in all alcoholic beverage advertisements regarding the risks of alcohol consumption, such as drinking during pregnancy and drinking and driving.

Remember: It pays to express yourself. Write to a legislator today stating your concerns about youth alcohol problems. Suggest some of the solutions listed in this chapter.

Resources

Organizations

Bureau of Alcohol, Tobacco and
   Firearms
650 Massachusetts Avenue, N.W.
Washington, D.C. 20226
(202) 927–7777
Write to protest noncompliance with statutes and codes.

National Clearinghouse for Alcohol
   and Drug Information
P.O. Box 2345
Rockville, MD 20847
(301) 468–2600
(800) 729–6686
The taped message will give you options; you can also order brochures and posters.

National Council on Alcoholism and
   Drug Dependence
12 West 21st Street
New York, NY 10010
(212) 206–6770
(800) NCA–CALL
Call to find your local affiliate and to order an information packet.

National Families in Action
2296 Henderson Mill Road, #300
Atlanta, GA 30345
(404) 934–6364
Ask for a free information packet on drugs and alcohol.

To Obtain Beer Advertising Codes

The Beer Institute
1225 I Street, N.W., Suite 825
Washington, D.C. 20005
(202) 737–BEER

Chapter 17

Help a Kid Kick Drugs

For kids under twenty-one, there is no difference between alcohol or other drug *use* and *abuse*. Use of these substances by young people puts their psychological, intellectual, and social functioning at risk. More than 4.6 million teenagers, or one-third of all American teens, have serious health, school, legal, or social difficulties related to their use of alcohol and other drugs.

—U.S. Department of Health and Human Services

Know the Facts

We don't really want to believe that our children could be using illicit drugs. We are so busy worrying about our jobs, our insurance, our child care, our taxes—just keeping our lives together—that we hardly have time to notice that our child, or a child we care about, has changed. But it is happening all the time.

- Over half of America's high school seniors have used an illicit drug at some time. An alphabet soup of drugs is readily available to our children even in grade-school playgrounds—PCP, cocaine, MDMA, LSD, mescaline, marijuana, speed, crack.
- Over 60% of adult addicts start using drugs during their adolescent years, when experimentation is part and parcel of growing up.
- Drug use among youth crosses all racial, social, and economic boundaries. But in some of our poorest urban communities, drugs have taken over. Crack, a particularly addictive and potent form of cocaine, is cheap and readily accessible and is destroying many neighborhoods and lives.
- In many major cities, 10% of babies are born already exposed to drugs; in some hospitals the number is much higher. A recent study says the care and treatment of cocaine-damaged babies costs our country $500 million per year.

What You Can Do
to Help a Kid Kick Drugs . . .

. . . At Home

Reach out to a kid who is abusing drugs. First, learn these common signs of drug abuse developed by the National Crime Prevention Council:

- withdrawal from previous interests, friends, or family members
- decline in academic performance
- reluctance to talk about new friends, or secretive phone calls
- unexplained absence from home or school
- periods of erratic behavior, excessive mood swings
- reduced energy, self-esteem, and enthusiasm
- frequent incidents of dishonesty
- defensive reactions to questions about substance use
- poor coordination, slurred speech, bloodshot eyes, extreme agitation, impaired judgment, inability to concentrate, lapses in memory

If a youngster you know has any of these signs, get involved. You may find that these are just signs of growing up, but it could be more serious. If the problem does not go away, find a drug treatment specialist in your community. Use your United Way, Yellow Pages, pediatrician, local hospital, school personnel, or other community agency to find professional help for the child.

Here's what one family did to help their son kick drugs: Rick was 15 years old, a B+ student, and an avid high school baseball player. Gradually, his parents noticed that he had been hanging out in his room instead of playing ball. After a few months, his grades dropped dramatically. They knew the signs, and they suspected he might be using drugs.

They determined to do something about it. Instead of confronting Rick with his drug use and screaming at him, they started talking to their son. In fact, they became relentless in their attempts to become more involved in his activities. Rick told his parents they were "in his face." They replied, "We love you and are concerned about you." They helped him with his homework, they planned more trips together, and they supported his involvement in new after-school activities. They also changed some of their own parental behavior: They started talking

about their own feelings; they were less likely to have cocktails after work; and they spent less time at their jobs. As gradually as it had begun, his drug use ended.

Remember: Don't give up easily. Denial is one of the significant dynamics in drug abuse. The parent will say, "Oh, it's just a phase he's going through." Even more difficult is denial on the part of the adolescent, who usually will say, "I don't do it," or "it's no big deal."

. . . In Your Community

Hold a crack baby.   Many cities have started programs for pregnant women addicted to crack. These programs often need volunteers. Find the program in your community by calling your local United Way agency or your local children's hospital. Some hospitals in urban areas need people to simply hold the babies, which can be very rewarding for you and the baby.

Be a role model.   It takes a special temperament to work with a troubled (most often angry or depressed) teenager. You probably know if this type of work would be right for you. If you had serious problems you had to overcome, you might be able to pass on some lessons and some understanding to a young person.

Help take back territory from drug dealers.   People are sick and tired of drugs dominating so many communities. **All over America, ordinary citizens are starting to take action and take back their communities.** And it's working—whether it is getting rid of a single crack house, or making the local grocery store a safe place to enter. Small goals can lead to broader efforts.

> **Take back the neighborhood!** In San Francisco, neighbors formed a group called Neighbors in Action to take back a park that for many years had been the center of drug dealing and violence. They held community forums, invited representatives of the police department, the recreation and parks department, and the mayor's office, and put these officials on the hot-seat. They organized neighborhood clean-up days. They got the recreation department to assign staff to the park, the police department to get off-duty cops to help with athletic programs, and they started a neighborhood watch program. After months of effort, they got the district attorney to take action against the crack house across the street from the park. Today, children play in the park and the dealers are gone. The effort brought people together to work on other problems.

Monitor your school's drug policies.   According to a federal law passed in 1990 (Drug-Free Schools and Community Act), every school must have an antidrug policy and drug education program or lose federal funds. They must make a written copy available to parents and students. Find out your school's policies. If they don't make sense, work to have them amended. If they are not being fully implemented, bring this to the attention of your local school board.

Support health education and values clarification from kindergarten through high school.   Drug education should focus on the social influences that led to drug abuse. Much drug education has not proven effective because it is not integrated into the child's school experiences, and it focuses on scare tactics. Fortunately, some effective curricula are being developed that focus on self-esteem, rather than scaring kids. For ideas about in-school or community drug programs, contact the National Crime Prevention Council (see Resources).

Urge your police and education departments to declare a drug-free zone around the school. Many communities have successfully limited drugs close to schools. When a drug-free zone policy is declared, police monitor the area very closely.

Get your community group or school to sponsor drug-free parties and other youth activities. An increasing number of schools and communities are sponsoring activities for young people, such as pizza nights and exciting field trips, that are free of alcohol and illicit drugs. One particularly successful event is a drug-free end-of-the-year dance or Senior Prom. The parties are very exciting—they often last all night—but they abide by certain rules. The keys to success are great food, great music, great location or decorations, and great activities. In other words, make the party a *big event*, not just the usual routine. The Grad Nite Foundation has compiled a how-to book and video on how to organize an alcohol-free and drug-free graduation night celebration (see Resources for information).

Join the Public Debate: Stop Drug Abuse

All levels of government have finally taken note of the drug problem. In 1986 the federal government declared a war on drugs. So far, the majority of money for that war has been spent on law enforcement and international drug control. In 1992, only 27% was spent on drug education and drug treatment. If this concerns you, contact your congressional representative to urge a shift in priorities.

Kids are using, stealing, and dying from drugs. I see it every day. Kids live in bad places, and need to get away. They don't have money to take trips or move. Dope takes you away—for a while, anyway. Hey, kids need good food, clothes, a good place to live, schools where people don't carry guns—you know.

—15-year-old boy

Resources

See the Resources for chapter 16 for more information on drugs.

Organizations

Bureau for At-Risk Youth
645 New York Avenue
Huntington, NY 11743
(800) 99–YOUTH
This group has a diverse and extensive catalogue of brochures, books, videotapes, games, stickers, and posters on drug and alcohol prevention, pregnancy prevention, child abuse, parenting, AIDS, and self-esteem.

Grad Nite Foundation
3090 Pullman
Costa Mesa, CA 92626
(714) 549–1919
Ask for their videotape and workbook on planning a drug-free bash for kids ($65.00).

National Crime Prevention Council
   (see Multi-Issue Resources)
Ask for posters, booklets, pamphlets, action kits, and other materials (some free) on drug prevention.

Chapter 18

Make Children's Health Care a Right

In this hemisphere only Bolivia and Haiti have lower immunization rates [than the United States] for their children. Our nation is the only industrialized nation in the entire world that does not guarantee childhood vaccination for all children.

—President Bill Clinton

Know the Facts

It's terrible to feel angry at your child for getting sick. But when you don't have health insurance, you can't help it. Especially over the weekend. At least during the week, my child can go to the school clinic for free.

—Mother without health insurance

- Almost 12 million children are not covered by health insurance—and most schools don't have clinics.
- People in the United States will spend almost $1 trillion on health care in 1993—more than the entire budgets of most nations in the world. This is a full 14% of our GNP—a greater portion than any other country in the world, and over $3,000 each year for every man, woman, and child. . . .

. . . And yet we can't even provide the most basic preventive health care to all our children. **What's wrong with this picture?**

To begin, invest 30 seconds to brief yourself on the health-care crisis for America's children:

- One-quarter of U.S. infants and 40% of all African-American and Hispanic infants in the United States are born to mothers who received inadequate prenatal care.

99

- Over a quarter of a million low-birthweight children are born in the United States every year. They are at high risk for death or permanent disabilities. Thirty other countries—including Costa Rica, Jordan, Greece, Egypt, Saudi Arabia, and Singapore—have better statistics on this than we do.

It is shocking that American children face problems that are typical of third world countries. It's shocking that these problems also exist in the United States—especially since basic health care to children is inexpensive and cost-effective: **Every dollar invested in immunizations saves $10 in medical costs associated with care for children with vaccine-preventable conditions.**

Why doesn't every American child get basic health care? Virtually all other industrialized countries, many not as wealthy as the United States, see health care as a universal right for children.

- **Doctors are not where they are needed.** Despite an overabundance of doctors, not enough work in poor communities or are willing to sign on poor patients. Inner cities and rural areas get short-changed.
- **Low-income families can't pay out-of-pocket for health care.** A typical kindergarten exam costs $250—nearly 20% of one month's income for a family of three with an annual income of $16,500 (150% of the 1992 federal poverty level). Preventive health services represent an inexpensive investment for a society, but they are a significant portion of the resources of low-income, and even moderate-income, families.
- **Free clinics** do not exist in many communities; when they do they are overburdened, underfunded, and often not open when people need them.
- **Health care for children and pregnant women receives only a small portion of our health-care budget.** Newly appointed Surgeon General Joycelyn Elders, M.D., has said that "Ninety percent is spent on people during the last month of life. We pay for people dying, not for health. Someone said that the most expensive day of your life is the day you die."

What You Can Do . . .

. . . To Help a Child Receive Needed Health Services

Help underwrite an uninsured child's health-care needs.
Some communities have developed innovative insurance programs: individuals and organizations make a contribution toward the cost of insurance premiums, and these are matched by corporations or insurance companies. Blue Cross has the largest such program. Ask your health department or a private insurer if such a program exists in your community.

Volunteer to help at a clinic for low-income children. Your community probably has at least one clinic for low-income families. These clinics, operated by hospitals, health departments, or nonprofits, are frequently understaffed and overworked, and would appreciate your energy. For example, you might offer child care or transportation to parents who would otherwise be unable to keep appointments, or simply make a telephone call to remind someone of an appointment.

Encourage your family pediatrician to accept children who are covered by public insurance. Increasingly, doctors are restricting their practices to children with private health insurance (and then, sometimes only certain plans.) As a result, more and more children with public insurance, such as Medicaid, are unable to get care. Yet if all doctors devoted at least 10% of their practice to such children, the current Medicaid doctor shortage would be stemmed, if not eliminated.

Help a sick child. The most common volunteer activity in America today is hospital volunteer work, much of which is done with children. Hospitals can be very scary and lonely places for children, and there are many ways for you to help. For example, familiar books and fun stories can reduce boredom and make a hospital stay a bit more pleasant. You might bring books to young patients, collect secondhand books to give to the hospital, or even make arrangements with the local library for a hospital loan program.

. . . To Increase Availability of Health Care

Learn about the child health needs of your community. Get started by asking a school nurse or a pediatrician about the health of children in your community. Visit a local clinic. See whether it is open when people need it, and what it is like to get care there.

Join—or start—a child health watch project. . . . The Children's Defense Fund (CDF) has organized Child Watch Visitation Programs all over the country. Citizen volunteers educate policy makers by arranging visits to children's programs and hospital wards, and organizing briefings on children's issues.

In Philadelphia local community groups, under the auspices of Philadelphia Advocates for Children and Youth, go door to door to identify families who need health care and then help them get the care they need. Their project, called Child Health Watch, collects the data, learns the problems, and then speaks out for the city's children. Call CDF for help getting Child Watch started (see Resources).

Organize an "Adopt-a-Clinic" program. Work with your church or synagogue, social or civic group, or workplace to direct financial and human resources toward a clinic that serves disadvantaged children. You might raise money for a new piece of equipment, help with outreach or public education, or provide on-site day care.

Help a community organization to start a public awareness campaign about health-care needs of children. Many families do not know what resources are available to them, or even the basics about well-baby care.

Here are some things you can do:

- **Order the videotape "Before It's Too Late, Vaccinate."** Developed by pediatricians, this videotape helps parents understand the importance of and overcome fears about vaccination. Show it at a PTA meeting or other group of parents.
- **Contact your local Kiwanis Club** about organizing a child health promotion event in your community. Kiwanis International has published an excellent series, *Young Children: Priority One,* which directs local clubs in health awareness and other child advocacy activities.
- **Advocate placing clinics where they are most accessible** to needy parents and children. Insist that your community provide child care, family-friendly hours, and outreach. One cost-effective strategy would be to urge a local business to provide vans (mobile clinics) that go to high-need neighborhoods to screen children and give prenatal care.

Support school-based health care. Urge school officials to have clinics in local high schools. The cost of a school-based clinic can be as low as $100 per child per year.

Join the Public Debate: Work for Health-Care Reform

Get the facts.

Now that the Clinton Administration has put health care at the top of its agenda, it is essential that all concerned citizens understand what type of reforms are needed to provide care for our children. We will all have the opportunity to pass judgment on the many proposals that will be put forward. Don't opt out. Study the list below, and judge each proposal by whether it meets these criteria.

1. **Coverage for all essential children's benefits.** Children's health-care needs are different from adults'. Make sure basic coverage includes health, vision, hearing, dental, and developmental assessments at regular, specified intervals; follow-up and all necessary treatment; and outreach and support services, such as transportation and home visiting.

2. **Guarantee of affordability.** There should be no requirements of contributions for well-child exams, immunizations, and other preventive pediatric services; full subsidization of other costs for low-income families; and sliding-scale costs for moderate income families.

3. **Continuous coverage.** Changes in family circumstances, such as employment, should not interrupt coverage.

4. **No exclusions of children with preexisting conditions.** Often health insurers won't provide coverage for people who are already sick—the ultimate Catch-22 in medical care.

5. **Culturally appropriate care providers, when needed.** Many parents cannot obtain care for their children because medical personnel don't speak their language or understand their customs or special needs.

6. **Cost-containment measures.** Cost-saving measures must be equally applied to all income groups, not just poor children.

Get involved.   Many groups are now working on health-care reform. Get on the mailing list and learn about the burgeoning health movement. Encourage organizations in your community to endorse the health-care principles listed above and to support proposals that will meet the needs of America's children.

Resources

Organizations

American Academy of Pediatrics
P.O. Box 927
Elk Grove, IL 60009
(708) 981–6758
Send for the videotape *Before It's Too Late, Vaccinate* ($4.00) and other educational materials.

Children's Defense Fund
(see Multi-Issue Resources)
Ask about how to start a Child Watch Visitation Program in your community.

Coalition for National Health
    Reform and Access to Care for the
    Underserved,
c/o National Association of
Community Health Centers
133 D New Hampshire, N.W.,
    Suite 122
Washington, D.C. 20036
(202) 659–8008
National coalition of activists and health providers.

Healthy Mothers, Healthy Babies
    Coalition
409 12th Street, S.W., Room 309
Washington, D.C. 20024-2188
(202) 863–2485
(800) 673–8444, ext. 2458
Ask how you can get connected to local and state organizations.

Kiwanis International
3636 Woodview Trace
Indianapolis, IN 46268-3196
(317) 875–8755

Ask how you can make contact with your local Kiwanis chapter. Send for the *Young Children: Priority One* publication series on what local chapters can do to promote child health.

March of Dimes
Campaign for Healthier Babies
1275 Mamaroneck Avenue
White Plains, NY 10605
(914) 428–7100
Ask for a packet on the Campaign; they can also connect you to a local or regional network.

Neighbor to Neighbor
2601 Mission Street, Suite 400
San Francisco, CA 94110
(415) 824–3355
Nationwide campaign for single-payer, universal health care.

Universal Health Care Action
    Network
1800 Euclid Avenue, Suite 318
Cleveland, OH 44115
(216) 566–8100
A nationwide single-payer coalition.

Publications

Maternal and Child Health Framework for Analyzing Health-Care Reform Plans, booklet produced by the Association of Maternal and Child Health Programs. To order, call (202) 775–0436.

Chapter 19

Understand Why Kids Run Away

Everyone in this world is not perfect. You don't know what we've lived with—there are 13 year olds that lived with drunk fathers that beat 'em and cursed 'em. People should ask us. Listen to us, but they don't. They don't care because we don't mean nothing.

—16-year-old runaway

Know the Facts

Maria is 14, and hasn't had a responsible person to look after her since she was nine. When Maria got home one night, her mother had disappeared—her stepfather said her mother left town with a bum she met in a bar. Maria stayed in an aunt's spare room for a few days, but then the aunt kicked her out. She dropped out of school for three months. She has fading bruises on the backs of her legs from where her stepfather beat her with a belt when he was drunk.

The police brought Maria to a youth shelter. She is one of America's 1 million youth who run away from home each year. To understand why kids run away, it helps to understand the myths and truths of their situation.

- MYTH: Kids run away because they don't like their parents' rules. They are "beyond parental control" and should be punished.

- TRUTH: **Runaway youth are victims:** two-thirds of all runaways who seek shelter have been physically or sexually abused by a parent. One-quarter come from homes where at least one parent abuses drugs; another 20% have an alcoholic parent. Many runaways are actually "throwaways"—young people who have been kicked out or abandoned by their parents.

- MYTH: Runaway kids are not "our community's" responsibility. They should go back where they belong.

- TRUTH: **Runaway children are from all socioeconomic backgrounds:** 39% from poor families, 34% from working-class families, and 27% from middle- and upper-class families. They are boys and girls of all races. If they do not receive help, they will live on the streets in ever-deteriorating health. If they are sent home without some resolution of their problems, they will simply leave again.

- MYTH: Runaway kids are on a lark.
- TRUTH: **Kids who live on the streets live amidst violence, drug abuse, and prostitution**—in the parts of our cities where most adults dare not go. They are frightened much of the time, and frequently victimized.

- MYTH: The real "victims" are the thousands of abducted little children—whose bodies "litter the countryside."
- TRUTH: **Most children who are considered "abducted" have actually been kidnapped by a parent fighting for custody.** This country has been terrified for years about little kids being abducted by strangers. Pictures of missing children appear everywhere—even on milk cartons. Actually, the numbers that so frighten people have been proved false. Rather than the 5,000 undocumented dead children a year we are told about, there are really 50 to 150 each year—and these are almost all teenagers. For these children and their families, the tragedy is beyond measure. Nevertheless, the facts do not warrant public hysteria about the kidnapping of young children.

What You Can Do to Help Runaway Kids . . .

. . . At Home

Help a runaway youth get help. Runaways are running *away* from something, not toward something. Once they get away to a strange part of town or to a new city, they are lost and desperate. Children who are

reached early on, before they become hardened to street life, are much more responsive to help. That is why the National Runaway Switchboard was established. This national 800 number (see Resources) is staffed by sensitive adults skilled in dealing with troubled youth. Kids who call get crisis counseling and assistance in getting to a safe shelter near where they are. If you see a child who is an obvious runaway (at a bus station, for example), reach out. You can listen to her story and let her know where she can get help. Encourage her to call the runaway hot line. The Switchboard will send you pocket-sized cards with their number and other information that you can then pass on to needy youngsters.

Volunteer in a program for runaway kids. Consult your United Way, telephone book, or the National Network for Runaway and Youth

Services for the runaway program nearest you. Like all runaway programs, it will be underfunded. As a volunteer you can do anything from "hang out" with the kids, to chaperone an outing, to organize a fund-raiser. The most important thing you can do is just listen to the kids' stories.

. . . In Your Community

Support the shelter for runaways in your community. Runaway kids should not be treated as criminals. If there is no home for runaways in your community, the police will have to resort to finding a reason to have these kids locked in the detention center. Advocate for community-based programs for runaway youth.

Urge your community to take responsibility. Runaways are sometimes referred to as "illegal aliens in their own land." They fall into a never-never land in the social service system. Most authorities claim they are not legal residents of the community, or that they are the responsibility of the parent—and no one else. If you don't urge your community to provide services to these kids, they will simply go without help.

Join the Public Debate: Oppose Criminalizing Runaway Children

The legal definition of runaway is "any person under the age of 18 who runs away from home for at least one night without parental permission." The use of the word "permission" implies blame to the child; yet most leave home out of desperation. In the 1970s the federal government recognized that runaway youth were most likely victims of family problems, and recommended against locking them up. Today, many state legislatures are once again trying to criminalize runaway behavior. Decades of locking these kids up did not help—and in fact damaged many children. It was double punishment.

Love me for what's inside of me . . . this is who I am.

—Runaway girl, age 13

Resources

Organizations

National Network of Runaway and
    Youth Services
1319 F Street, N.W., Suite 401
Washington, D.C. 20004
(202) 783–7949
This is a clearinghouse for
information on runaway youth.

Switchboards

National Runaway Switchboard
(800) 621–4000
This is a 24-hour hot line for runaway
kids and searching parents; send for
free posters and cards.

Publications

*How to Talk So Kids Will Listen: How
to Listen So Kids Will Talk*, by Adele
Faher and Elaine Mazlich. New
York: Avon, 1982 ($9.00). To order,
call (800) 747–8802. You can also
order a videotape series and
workshop kit to go with the book.

Chapter 20

Bring Young and Old Together

I think people who live a long time do somehow learn patience, and they teach little children patience also. Volunteering to help with young people is one of the most wonderful things. I have some friends who have enriched their own lives by being part of a program called Foster Grandparents. They don't have any of their own grandchildren handy, so they are grandparents to somebody else's.

—Pete Seeger

Know the Facts

What could be more natural than a child sitting on a grandparent's knee? Or a person who has experienced more than 60 years of life helping a youngster puzzle out the next step in looking for a job? Or a teenager escorting an elderly person home safely?

Yet in our society, such "natural" moments are rare.

- We segregate old from young, and that is not only sad but foolish.
- We waste the untapped resources of the older generation, and deprive the generations coming up from benefiting from elders' patience, experience, wisdom, and delight in the younger generation.

The lives of both young and old are enriched by regular exchanges. Old people, segregated in nursing homes or "adult" apartment buildings, often miss the warmth and stimulation that comes from contact with children; young people (especially those from single-parent households, or whose families are in disarray) may not even know what it's like to have a stable, attentive older adult who is willing to spend time with them.

What You Can Do
to Get Young and Old Together

One program that exemplifies the mutual benefits of bringing young and old together is a telephone project called Grandma, Please, developed at Hull House in Chicago. When children come home to an empty house after school and just need a little friendly conversation, they call and ask for "Grandma, Please." Grandma is a "mobility-limited" senior who works out of her own home through a centralized switchboard. The program allows two otherwise isolated people to come together. The child receives the undivided attention of a caring, nonjudgmental adult, and the senior volunteer enjoys the benefits of making contact and keeping in touch with the younger generation.

If you are a senior, there are a number of ways you can get involved—either on your own, or through a group. Here are some ideas that have worked:

- Grandmothers visit neonatal intensive care units, where they spend time touching and holding crack-addicted babies.
- Churches sponsor intergenerational celebrations, with shared activities such as bread-baking and quilt-making.
- Seniors visit day-care centers and libraries to read to children.
- Programs match older adults with families who are looking for an "adopted" aunt, uncle, or grandparent.
- Senior residential homes develop after-school programs right on the premises.
- Retired businesspeople offer their expertise to teenagers looking for jobs and to children's organizations.

- Older artists act as mentors and artists-in-residence to kindle and keep alive the creative spark in kids.
- Seniors lend their expertise to overburdened teachers, as guest speakers, tutors, and curriculum advisers.

Seniors: Stand up for kids! Seniors have a lot of power. That's because politicians fear the senior vote. One in five voters belongs to the influential American Association of Retired Persons (AARP).

- While poverty among the elderly is declining and is below the national average, poverty among children has been skyrocketing.
- Every senior is assured of basic health care. Every child is not.
- Federal expenditures for seniors in America are five times the expenditures for children. During the 1980s, when programs for children were cut, spending on the elderly rose over 50%. Yet there are half as many people over age 65 as under age 18.

Today, more and more seniors are realizing that they must now use their power to champion children.

Remember: The strongest way to bring young and old together in America is to lend the political power of seniors to children.

Resources

Organizations

Generations United
c/o Child Welfare League of America
440 First Street, N.W., Suite 310
Washington, D.C. 20001-2085
(202) 638–2952
Ask for information on intergenerational programs in your community. This is a national coalition sponsored by AARP, National Council on Aging, Child Welfare League of America, and the Children's Defense Fund.

Chapter 21

Make Your Neighborhood Safe for Kids

In the last year there have been shootouts at parties, drug dealers killing people because of the situations they're in, violence on buses, and that makes me scared to even leave the house, because now you can't have the fun you used to when you were younger. Times have changed.

—From a letter to a mayor written by a 15-year-old

Know the Facts

Our society glorifies violence. By the time a child has completed sixth grade, he or she will have seen 8,000 murders on television and 100,000 other acts of violence. Even children's toys are violent—we're all familiar with water guns styled after submachine guns, and video games that give points for enemies killed.

Yet, for some reason, we like to think that our children will be protected from violence. They are not.

- An American child is 5 to 13 times more likely to be murdered than a child in any other industrialized country. In fact, the death of children has become so prevalent in inner cities that there is mounting pressure in many communities to have schools take out burial insurance on their young students.
- Teens are twice as likely as adults, and ten times more likely than the elderly, to be victims of violent crime. One-third of our children fear an attack on the way to school.
- A study of fifth-graders in New Orleans showed that over half had been victims of violence; over 90% had witnessed violence; 40% had seen dead bodies; and 70% had seen weapons being used.

And now children are not only the victims of violence, sometimes they are the perpetrators. Perhaps the greatest violence-promoting change that has occurred since we were young is the availability of guns. Half of all households have at least one gun. Easy access to guns has created deadly consequences for children, particularly those living in poverty.

- We are all alarmed and frightened about the rise of gangs, yet gangs are an old urban problem—remember *West Side Story?* The major difference between gangs 30 years ago and gangs today is simply the availability of guns.
- It is not uncommon for high school students in inner cities to pass through metal detectors as they enter school—at a cost of $400 per detector to underfunded schools.
- Five percent of kids surveyed by the Centers for Disease Control had carried a gun to school in the past month; 20% carried a weapon of some kind.

What You Can Do . . .

. . . In Your Neighborhood

Make your house a safe house for kids. A few years ago, two women in Albany, California, decided to establish a Block Parent program. Block Parents have signs posted in their windows, indicating that their homes are safe havens for children who are ill, injured, endangered, or frightened. The program works closely with the police. Information about the program is posted in all schools, and fliers are sent home to parents. Start a safe house program if your community does not have one. Contact the National McGruff House Network for assistance (see Resources).

Join a neighborhood watch group. Many neighborhoods in our country no longer have the luxury of a friendly police officer on foot patrol. Members of neighborhood watch groups help out by keeping a sharp eye out for suspicious activities in their neighborhood. Signs are posted in the neighborhood to warn potential wrongdoers that they are being watched. For more information on this and other crime-prevention programs, contact the National Crime Prevention Council (see Resources).

Help kids take back their parks.   Parks, traditionally safe areas for kids to play in, have grown increasingly dangerous in recent years. In 1988 in New York City, 25 members of Youth Force decided to take back three midtown Manhattan parks from the drug dealers, addicts, and prostitutes who had been frightening kids and families away. The program, Take Back the Park, is run by kids and for kids. After their first outreach effort, over 1,200 kids followed the group into the parks instead of hanging out on the street. Suggest to local youth groups or law enforcement agencies ways kids themselves can fight crime. Contact Kids Against Crime for ideas (see Resources).

. . . In Your Community

Join a conflict-resolution program.   Community or school conflict resolution groups are where ordinary citizens create a forum for the settlement of disputes. In Richmond, California, a poor community with bad police/community relations, youth and senior citizens work together to respond to potentially violent incidents. (They do not intervene in actively violent situations.) With the cooperation of local police, teams of youths and seniors are equipped with radio-band scanners and beepers so that they can respond to calls for assistance. They try to reach a peaceful resolution. Contact the Community Boards program for information on how to initiate or run such a program (see Resources).

Volunteer to be a hall monitor at a public school. In some tough schools, the presence of an interested adult can make a difference. In Oakland, California, some parents work as hall monitors in the high schools that their kids go to in order to help deal with violence.

Become a Mad Dad. Eddie Staton of Omaha, Nebraska, decided one day that "If something was going to be done to solve the violence, it was going to be done by us." With a few friends, he started by painting over the neighborhood graffiti. "We didn't go to the city council, state senator, or anybody—we just did it." Youth started to rally around to see what was happening, and so began one of the most amazing grassroots organizations this country has seen in recent years. Mad Dads now has chapters across the country and has been featured in the national media. In Omaha they have regular weekend patrols, outreach in schools, neighborhood cleanup projects, and much more. The original graffiti "artists" have become their ardent allies, and gang activity in Omaha has been reduced by over 90%!

Frustrated by the violence in his community of West Ocala, Florida, another mad dad and his four daughters started by standing in front of city hall with signs highlighting the problem. This single act turned into a community-wide organization involving hundreds of individuals, who are now involved in street patrols, mentoring, and tutoring.

These two examples illustrate what can be done by individuals who just decide one day that it is time to get involved.

Urge your police department to arrange a "gang summit." Summits have reduced gang violence in many communities. Gang members, community residents, and police come together to deal with the problem. Tension between gangs can often be dealt with by talking, rather than with aggressive law enforcement.

Join the Public Debate: Fight for Sensible Firearms Policies.

The easy availability of handguns has created deadly consequences for young Americans, particularly those living in poverty with no jobs or job prospects. Most Americans strongly support stricter laws controlling guns. Here's one person's idea: In 1991, at the suggestion of one passionate child advocate, San Francisco enacted a gun amnesty program. Residents were paid $50 for every gun they turned in to the police. No questions were asked, and so many guns were turned in that the initial allocation of $10,000 ran out within the first week of the program. Similar programs have succeeded in St. Louis, Minneapolis, and other cities.

Resources

Organizations

Alliance Against Violence in
 Entertainment for Children
17 Greenwood Street
Marlboro, MA 01752
(508) 481–6926
This volunteer, grassroots network is dedicated to reducing TV violence.

Center to Prevent Handgun Violence
1225 Eye Street, N.W., Suite 1100
Washington, D.C. 20005
(202) 289–7319
Send for their excellent, free educational materials on children and guns.

Community Board Program, Inc.
1540 Market Street, Suite 490
San Francisco, CA 94102
(415) 552–1250
Ask for information about this school program, which teaches kids to be conflict managers; provides technical assistance nationwide.

Kids Against Crime
1700 North East Street
San Bernardino, CA 92405
(714) 882–1344
Ask for information on getting kids involved in crime prevention, graffiti cleanup, peer support, gang prevention. Contact them to find out how to start a chapter in your community.

Mad Dads, Inc.
2221 W. 24th Street
Omaha, NE 68110
(402) 451–3500.
The dedicated leaders of this organization can help you start a Mad Dads chapter to work to stop violence in your community.

National Crime Prevention Council
  (see Multi-Issue Resources)
Ask for information on all aspects of neighborhood safety programs, from neighborhood watches to gang prevention. Send for posters, booklets, educational kits, newsletters; ask how you can find a crime prevention program near you.

The National McGruff House
  Network
1879 South Main Street, Suite 180
Salt Lake City, UT 84115
(801) 486-8768
Ask for information on how to start a safe home program, or a McGruff Truck program with your utility company.

Publications

Deadly Consequences: How Violence Is Destroying Our Teenage Population and a Plan to Begin Solving the Problem, by Deborah Prothrow-Stith, M.D. New York: HarperCollins, 1991.

Chapter 22

Lobby for Kids at Budget Time

Our tax structure gives more incentive to raising race horses than it does to raising children.

—Sylvia Hewlett, *When the Bough Breaks*

Know the Facts

Budget-making is nothing more than a political process of satisfying the most powerful and most aggressive constituencies. That's why, for the past 30 years, the portion of our public budgets spent on children has declined steadily, while the needs of children have increased. That's why, as the Children's Defense Fund tells us, every hour in 1992 our federal government managed to find $8.7 million to bail out the savings and loans, but only $1.8 million to provide health care to our children, whose health is worse than children in Canada, Hong Kong, Greece, and Spain.

- The United States gives less effective benefits to children than any other country in the Western industrialized world. In other countries, tax and other benefits lift most children out of poverty.
- In California the prison budget increased by 500% in the past 15 years, while funding to education was cut by $70 billion.

In the 1980s children's services were cut $40 billion, while the defense establishment gained $1.9 trillion. As a popular bumper sticker says, "It will be a great day when our schools get all the money they need and the Air Force has to hold a bake sale to buy a bomber." According to the United Nations, the United States spends 23% of its budget on defense—France, Canada, China, and Germany spend 7% or 8%.

Every year the average American gives thousands of dollars to the government in taxes. Normally, we would not be casual about such a major investment. Yet for most Americans, the annual budget process of their city, state, or national government remains a complete mystery. Creating the budget is the most important task of our elected officials.

This is when they tell us whether they are going to deliver on their promises and their obligation to all citizens.

The budget comes from your paycheck. For the sake of our children, become informed about how your tax dollars are being spent. If you focus on just one aspect of the budget, you can begin to make sure your tax dollars work better for the benefit of children. Vow not to let another paycheck arrive without committing yourself to exercising some citizen oversight.

ONE-MINUTE BUDGET BRIEFING:
ALL YOU NEED TO KNOW TO MAKE A DIFFERENCE

- Each level of government has important responsibilities in meeting the needs of children. Federal and state governments share responsibility for health care, income maintenance, foster care, food, and job training for children and youth; local and state governments share responsibility for education, child care, homeless services, recreation, and libraries.

- The budget is usually drafted by the executive branch of government, and reviewed and passed by the legislative branch. The executive functions are carried out behind closed doors; legislative functions are public. Work by the legislature is done in committees and subcommittees, which is where public input is usually heard and reviewed.

- Most local and state governments operate on a fiscal year that begins in July. Mayors, governors, and so on develop budgets in the winter. Legislatures review them in the spring, and generally budgets are approved in late June.

- The federal government, however, is on an October-to-October fiscal calendar. The president usually presents the budget to Congress in January, and Congress debates through the summer—sometimes longer. Congress first establishes general parameters (budget resolution), and then specific appropriations.

- Many paid lobbyists follow the budget process on an hour-by-hour basis. They corner key decision-makers (elected and staff) regularly. Legislators know the difference between lobbyists and constituents. Lobbyists have money. Constituents have votes. Our democracy is now in a life-and-death struggle over which

will prevail. Much remains to be done to dilute the power of paid lobbyists, but constituents *can* win!
- Both branches of government are sensitive to public opinion regarding the budget, but generally the legislature is more sensitive.

WHERE DOES YOUR FEDERAL TAX DOLLAR GO?

- Defense: 21¢
- Social security: 19¢
- Interest: 13¢
- Medicare: 8¢
- Income security (other than that listed separately): 7¢
- Health: 6¢
- Commerce and housing credit: 6¢
- Federal employee retirement: 4¢
- Education, training, employment development, and social services: 3¢
- Unemployment compensation: 2¢
- Transportation: 2¢
- Veterans' benefits: 2¢
- International affairs: 1¢
- Natural resources and environment: 1¢
- Agriculture: 1¢
- Science, space, and technology: 1¢
- Administration of justice: 1¢
- General government: 1¢
- Energy: 0.5¢
- Community development: 0.5¢

Memorize this mindboggling fact: The richest 1% of households will owe $43 billion less in federal taxes in 1993 than they would owe if they paid the same percentage of income in taxes as in 1977! That's enough money to end child poverty in America!

Copy or tear out this page. Use this information to fight for kids.

What You Can Do to Make
Children a Budgetary Priority

Don't be intimidated! You don't have to understand *any* of the numbers or *any* of the jargon to have your voice heard and your opinions make sense. Technical as it all sounds, it is really only about setting priorities; and if you know why you want children to be a priority, that is all you need to make a compelling budget argument.

Follow the news. Funding-related issues are frequently in the news. When you see an article about a local playground or library service being cut, read it and plan some kind of action. Bring the issue to the attention of your church or PTA, or post it on the bulletin board at work or at the laundromat. Write a letter of protest.

Write an annual budget letter to your Congress member. Two months before the budget is finalized (this will usually be in April in your city and state), let your legislators know that you want children to be a priority in the coming year's budget. If you are going to write only one letter to your Congress member, do it in January or February, when

"I guess we can't cut that program this year, can we?"

the official budget debate begins. Send a copy of your letter to the editor of your local newspaper. Often politicians pay more attention when the pressure is public, and they monitor the media closely.

Remember: If every registered voter wrote *one* letter a year to Congress about children, that would be more letters than they receive on all other issues combined. Overnight, this action would make children the highest, rather than the lowest, political priority.

Subscribe to a children's action newsletter. Several children's groups monitor the budget process closely (see Resources). They send out regular newsletters and action alerts, telling you exactly what children's items are in jeopardy (such as funding for childhood immunizations, schools, or summer jobs programs), and when and who to write or call. Get on the mailing list of national, state, and local groups. If you must pick only one, for $30 subscribe to *CDF Reports*, the monthly newsletter of the Children's Defense Fund.

Testify at the public budget hearing. Call City Hall to find out the dates of the public budget hearings on the issues of concern to you, such as the recreation department. The hearings will probably be in the spring. Be sure to find out when public testimony will be heard. Confirm this by phone at least once before going to a hearing—changes are made up to the last minute.

You may have to wait hours for your item; you may feel intimidated. You will no doubt be surrounded by professionals in suits with briefcases. But stick with it—you *will* have an impact—especially since so few people participate in budget hearings, and since you, unlike just about everyone else there, will not be representing a self-serving special interest group. If you take some friends—or better yet, if you take some children—your voice will be all the more powerful.

For the More Ambitious Child Advocate

One persistent and outraged person can truly make his or her voice heard on the local level, particularly if that person feels strongly about a particular children's service that should be in the budget. Here are some ideas.

Invite a budget-maker to a children's program. Begin early. Invite a city council member to visit a program you want to see in the budget, such as a day-care center. When the mayor of one city actually visited a program for sexually abused children, the budget for that program *was never cut again.*

Get help from community groups.　Enlist the help of civic or religious organizations in your community to advocate for your cause. Many groups, ranging in outlook from Kiwanis, to the League of Women Voters, to the Unitarian Church, to the Junior League, have made child advocacy a priority.

Use the media.　Find a newspaper or TV reporter interested in doing a story on the program you want funded (or don't want cut). Once the media starts making inquiries, you'll be surprised how quickly your issue gets to the top of the list of public officials.

Use drama.　One group had a volunteer Santa (a local actor) appear in the mayor's office with a group of children at Christmas to deliver a budget wish-list for the coming year. It was irresistible.

Remember: Now that Hillary Clinton, the former Chair of the Board of the Children's Defense Fund, is in the White House, and President Clinton is adamant about supporting children's programs, elected officials all over are on notice to respond to children's concerns.

Resources

Federal Budgets

Children's Defense Fund
(see Multi-Issue Resources)
Ask about newsletters; first of the month action alert; "A Children's Defense Budget," an annual federal budget analysis; and *The State of America's Children*, annual report.

Child Welfare League of America
(see Multi-Issue Resources)
Send for regular newsletters on the state of children and the federal budget.

State Budgets

National Association of Child Advocates (see Multi-Issue Resources)
Ask for the names of budget-monitoring organizations in your state.

Local Budgets

National League of Cities
(see Multi-Issue Resources)
Ask about the "Children in Cities"
project, and for names of
organizations in your city.

Organizations

Campaign for New Priorities
(800) 92–ACTION
Use their toll-free number to send a
message to your elected
representatives about the need to
reduce defense spending and invest in
America. Be sure to give the name of
the organization you are calling!

Center on Budget and Policy Priorities
(see Multi-Issue Resources)
This is a think-tank on budget-related
issues.

Publications

*When the Bough Breaks: The Cost of
Neglecting Our Children*, by Sylvia
Ann Hewlett. New York:
HarperCollins, 1991.

Chapter 23

Fight for Car Seats, Helmets, and Smoke Detectors

Before you do anything else, strap your children in their car safety seats and quit smoking—then let's begin discussing other hazards for children.

—Advice of a leading pediatrician

Know the Facts

It is always a tragedy when a child gets hurt or dies. But it is a double tragedy when that injury or death could have easily been prevented. Unfortunately, this is very often the case.

- For children under 15, injuries account for more deaths than all diseases combined.
- Each year injuries take the lives of approximately 10,000 children under age 15. One child in four will suffer a preventable injury serious enough to require medical attention.
- The yearly costs of childhood injuries are estimated to exceed $7.5 billion.

Children depend on us. Young people do not have the power to make such decisions as the legal age to drive, the safety standards of bicycle helmets, or the availability of firearms. Children must depend on adults to protect them from many hazards and injury risks.

What You Can Do . . .

. . . To Ensure Safer Motor Vehicles

Support car seat loaner programs. Car seats reduce the risk of serious injuries to young children by as much as 70%. Although using a car seat is probably the single most important thing an adult can do to protect a child, many families can't afford car seats. Buy one for a needy family, or find out if your community has a car seat loaner program. If not, contact your local hospital, health department, or service club and urge them to establish one. Call the National Highway Traffic Safety Administration for information (see Resources).

Retrofit your car with three-point seat belts.   Three-point seat belts are much more effective than lap belts in the back seats of most cars. The National Highway Traffic Safety Administration can send you a retrofit kit.

. . . To Ensure Pedestrian Safety

Fight for speed limits, stop signs, and properly marked crosswalks.   Call your state highway department or local traffic department to insist they make an unsafe intersection or street safe for children. Then call again and again, until they do something. Enlist the help of neighbors, friends or teachers.

Be a crossing guard.   Crossing guards keep children safe on the way to school. Many crossing guard programs are run by volunteers.

. . . To Ensure Bicycle Safety

Start a bicycle helmet campaign.   Four out of five bicycle-related deaths are the result of injuries to the head. Bicycle helmets decrease head injury by about 85%. Urge your local police department, school system, or service club to run a campaign. Here are some strategies that work: issue "good" tickets—that can be redeemed for prizes—to kids wearing helmets; put in place policies that mandate bicycle helmet use; give away discount coupons for helmets through local distributors, such as Toys R Us; and organize fund raisers for helmet giveaways.

You can have an impact. The first law in the country requiring bicyclists under 16 to wear safety helmets was initiated by students and teachers in one high school. Spurred by the death of a fellow student, a group from Glenwood Middle School in Howard County, Maryland, coordinated the campaign that led to the passage of the law.

. . . To Prevent Fires and Burns

Install a smoke detector.   After you install your own smoke detector, give one to a friend! Smoke detectors prevent children (and their parents) from dying in fires. Then remember to check the battery each year.

Install a water-temperature control device.   Scald burn devices shut off the flow of water when the temperature becomes dangerous. They are easy to install onto your home water taps. Support legislation that would mandate scald burn devices in new construction.

. . . To Prevent Poisonings
Did you know that 90% of poisonings occur in the home? And that 95% of all accidental poisonings can be prevented?

Learn the phone number of your poison control center.   Post the number by your own phone and encourage people you know to keep it posted by their phones. Many poison control centers have free services, including a 24-hour hot line, community education programs, and health education materials. Urge your local radio and TV stations to air a public service announcement about the services provided by your poison control center.

Support regulation of products.   Child-resistant closures, annoying as they can be, have had a tremendous impact on reducing childhood poisonings. Advocate for such changes as packaging only small quantities, reducing prescription refills, and using formulations that are less lethal.

. . . To Control Firearms
Every two hours someone's child is killed with a loaded gun. The number of handguns in the United States has more than doubled in the past 20 years. Today, approximately 50% of U.S. households have a gun. Incredibly, 10,500 firearms *per day* are manufactured in the United States or are imported.

Become a gun control advocate.   Gun control is controversial in the United States, and many people erroneously think it's an all-or-nothing issue. Yet advocating for certain gun control measures—such as a ban on the manufacture and sale of handguns, a national waiting period to purchase firearms, and child safety locks—would prevent many of the needless deaths that result from firearm violence. Write to your elected officials and state your concerns about firearm violence.

Rid your house of guns.   This one's simple: When you remove guns from your house, you will immediately decrease the chances of someone in your family being shot. Guns in the home are 43 times more likely to kill a family member or friend than an intruder.

. . . To Prevent Drownings

Become a swimming pool watchdog.   Kids love pools, and they often drown in them. Childproof pool fencing, which completely surrounds the pool, is very effective in preventing drownings. Make sure that the public pools in your community meet safety standards and are properly staffed with lifeguards during all hours of operation.

From tragedy to action. After the drowning of her two-year-old daughter and the near-drowning of her year-old son, Nadina Riggsbee founded the Drowning Prevention Foundation. This coalition of parents of drowning victims, local pediatricians, and public health professionals had its first success with an ordinance in Contra Costa County, California, that required all backyard pools installed after 1984 to have at least one of three safety measures: fencing at least 4-1/2 feet high that completely surrounds the pool, plus a self-closing and self-latching gate; a pool safety cover; and an audible alarm on all home exits leading to the pool.

Resources

Organizations

Consumer Product Safety
  Commission
Publications Department
Washington, D.C. 20207
(800) 638–CPSC
Send for information about product safety, including playground safety; file product-safety complaints with them. Ask for their *Handbook for Public Playground Safety*, volume 1.

National Highway Traffic Safety
  Administration
(800) 424–9393
Call for information on seat belts.

National Safe Kids Campaign
111 Michigan Avenue, N.W.
Washington, D.C. 20010
(202) 939–4993
This is a national campaign sponsored by Johnson & Johnson to prevent childhood injuries. They have extensive public information materials, including videotapes, brochures, posters, fact sheets, and magazines, that discuss seat belts, burn prevention, bike helmets, and accident prevention.

Publications

Saving Children, by Hoover Wilson, et al. New York: Oxford University Press, 1991.

Chapter 24

Face the Fact that Children Get AIDS

I've had AIDS since I was fifteen. I got it
from sexual activity when I was thirteen.
You'd have to know my history to understand. I never thought about getting AIDS.
We thought it was gay cancer.

— 18-year-old young woman

Know the Facts

If you don't know someone who has AIDS, the chances are, tragically,
that you will. And that person may be a child:

- By the end of 1992, 5,000 children and youth in the United
  States had been diagnosed with AIDS. Between 10,000 and
  20,000 American children are infected with HIV, the virus associated with AIDS, and the numbers are rapidly growing.
- Most children with HIV—unlike Ryan White, the Indiana boy
  who first brought childhood AIDS to national attention—are
  not infected through a blood transfusion. They are exposed to
  the virus in the womb, or much later, as sexually active
  teenagers.
- Teenagers, especially boys, are increasingly at risk of contracting
  HIV. One reason is that teens often engage in risky behavior of all
  kinds, from experimenting with drugs and alcohol to "unsafe"
  sex. But it's also because far too many adults—swayed by false or
  misguided moralism, actively prevent young people from getting
  the protection and honest information they need.
- More than ten years into the AIDS epidemic, the needs of children and youth who suffer from the disease are still widely over-
  looked by government agencies, researchers, service providers
  and advocates.

- Perhaps the most devastating impact of the AIDS epidemic on children is the increasing number of children who are left motherless. By the end of the century, just a few more years, 80,000 American children will have lost their mothers to AIDS. This is a true social catastrophe.

What You Can Do to Help Kids Understand AIDS . . .

. . . At Home

Educate yourself. Let's face it: HIV/AIDS is a tough issue. There is still no known cure. HIV is associated with intimate, emotion-laden behavior like sex and drug use—difficult issues to discuss, especially with children and adolescents. But as a well-known AIDS activist slogan proclaims, "Silence = Death." It's time for every one of us to set aside our discomforts and biases in order to deal head-on with this epidemic.

Young people—even many adults!—need constant reassurance that HIV is *not* transmitted by casual or household contact. *You can hug, massage, feed, bathe, and care for a person with HIV without risk.* The virus is transmitted by a very limited range of unsafe sexual and drug-using practices—and it can be prevented when young people receive the information, skills, and encouragement they need to stay safe.

Remember: Survival and quality of life for children and youth with HIV improve dramatically with early identification of the virus and comprehensive health care.

Spread the word, not the disease. Talk to your own children about HIV and AIDS. You can get further information about HIV and AIDS from community organizations, health departments, libraries, bookstores—and from your own doctor or health worker. Contribute to prevention by starting up discussions with young people you are close to. Don't assume that children already know about AIDS, or that keeping the subject at bay will keep them safe.

Distribute AIDS information to friends, your PTA, members of your church or synagogue, or colleagues at work. Fact sheets and pamphlets are available from your local health department, AIDS organizations, and the groups listed in Resources.

. . . In Your Community

Support AIDS education in the schools.   Talk to your children's teachers, or call your school district. Find out what kinds of AIDS prevention and education activities they are offering to children and youth. Although the final responsibility rests with parents and families, you have the right to insist that school-age children learn about HIV prevention in their health education programs. If this isn't happening, talk to the school principal, as well as to school board members and other public officials.

JUST SAY NO TO CENSORSHIP:
DEFEND A CHILD'S RIGHT
TO LEARN THE FACTS ABOUT AIDS

Successful prevention strategies must be understandable, credible, relevant, and accessible to kids—and consistently reintroduced and repeated. This means that we have to meet children where they are, and it means facing the fact that many young people are sexually active or experimenting with drugs.

That's why a narrow, moralistic approach to AIDS education has become so dangerous. A one-dimensional message to "just say no" not only misses the point—it puts children at greater risk by leaving them ignorant about safe and unsafe behavior.

Be a volunteer.   Get involved in activities that support people with HIV and AIDS and the organizations that serve them. Most AIDS agencies are badly in need of volunteers, and will offer you training and support. You might be good at answering hot-line calls a few hours a week, or you could make a commitment to one child or parent by visiting regularly to talk and help with chores. Other agencies need volunteers to help with meal preparation and delivery, transportation, baby-sitting, or collecting donations of toys, games, books, clothes, gift certificates and other items.

"We're all in the same boat . . . and one of us has HIV."

Join the Public Debate:
Fight Discrimination

> Besides enduring the physical pain of the disease, most of these children face a great deal of emotional trauma and social isolation in their communities.
>
> —Geri Brooks, founder of Sunburst projects

Because AIDS is associated with sexuality (especially homosexuality) and with drug use, the disease is still widely considered to be somehow shameful—as though the person who is affected deserves what has happened. Bigoted AIDS "humor" is prevalent. Many families of people with HIV or AIDS still keep their experience a secret, for fear of how neighbors and colleagues will respond. Be a vocal advocate for fairness. Stop prejudice in its tracks by refusing to tolerate it. Show your friends and community that AIDS isn't something you're afraid to talk about honestly.

Dealing with HIV and AIDS is tough enough without having to worry about the barriers of discrimination and prejudice. Children and youth who face this disease have the right to enjoy full and productive lives, with equal access to education, recreation, housing, employment and other services. The federal Americans with Disabilities Act includes protections for people with AIDS—but it doesn't mean that discriminatory policies and attitudes have come to an end. Does your town or city government also have a nondiscrimination policy covering people with HIV and AIDS? How about your school district, recreation department, housing authority? Your workplace? Your child-care center? Ask—and if they don't, ask why not.

Remember: We can win the fight against AIDS—but only if each of us lends a hand, spreads the facts, and helps to keep our children safe.

Resources

Organizations

Pediatric AIDS Foundation
1311 Colorado Avenue
Santa Monica, CA 90404
(310) 395–9051
This national organization helps hospitals, researchers, students, and the public to confront the medical problems unique to children infected with HIV/AIDS.

Project AHEAD (Alliance for
    the Health of Adolescents)
375 Woodside Avenue
San Francisco, CA 94127
(415) 753–7786
This federally funded project on HIV/AIDS in adolescents and young adults has videotapes, brochures, manuals, and training guides for health and youth professionals, parents, and youth.

Sunburst National AIDS Project
148 Wilson Hill Road
Petaluma, California 94952
(707) 769–0169
This national project supports families with children with HIV/AIDS and other life-threatening illnesses. Send for their brochure, *Children with AIDS: Guidelines for Parents and Caregivers.*

Switchboards

National AIDS Information Hot Line
(800) 342–AIDS
(800) 344–SIDA (Spanish language)
(800) AIDS–TTY (For the hearing impaired)

Teaching AIDS Prevention
(800) 234–8336
This information line is staffed by and for teens.

Chapter 25

Get a Kid
Out of Jail
and Into College

Children who go unheeded are children who are
going to turn on the world that neglected them.

—Robert Coles

Know the Facts

Most juvenile corrections experts believe that the United States now
locks up more of its children than any other country in the world. This
is certainly a tragic reflection of our attitude toward youth, especially
since most of the incarcerated kids come from families that are abusive, neglectful, or impoverished. But in addition to destroying lives,
the juvenile justice system is costing a fortune: A year in a juvenile detention facility costs an average of $30,000 per child!

Here are the facts:

- Over half a million youth are incarcerated each year, a number
  that has increased by nearly 30% in the past decade. Two-thirds
  of the youth detained pose no threat to society, since they only
  committed minor or nonviolent offenses.
- With notable exceptions, locked juvenile institutions—jails—do
  nothing more than "hold" children, offering little in the way of
  rehabilitative services. Recidivism rates of 50% and 75% are not
  unusual. According to the U.S. Dept. of Justice, half of all youth
  are in overcrowded facilities.
- Youth are often victims of brutality by other youth and by staff
  in many juvenile correctional institutions. In 1990, 24,000 youth
  were injured in detention, 11,000 demonstrated suicidal behavior, and 10 juveniles actually killed themselves during their incarceration.
- 150 countries have signed the United Nations Convention on
  the Rights of the Child, adopted by the General Assembly in

1989. As of this writing, the United States is not one of those countries. One major reason: We refuse to oppose the death penalty for children. The United States has executed more juveniles than any nation except Iran and Iraq.

Saving kids from jail. One nationally recognized program for youth, the Omega Boys Club in San Francisco, routinely rescues children from the juvenile jail. The so-called worst kids are recruited for a club that functions as an extended family. Kids can go to the community center where the club meets every single day. They get food, help with homework, lots of encouragement, support, and individual attention, and exposure to career opportunities. "Hundreds of youth who were on the road to San Quentin are now in colleges across the country," says the club's founder.

What You Can Do
for Kids Who Are Locked Up

Take a tour of the juvenile detention facility. Somewhere in your community, troubled youth are being locked up. The fact that they have committed a crime signals that they need help. Find these kids by going to your local probation department and asking to visit the juvenile hall. If the probation authorities are reluctant to let you in, persist: It is a public institution and you are a taxpayer. It is very likely that the conditions you see will be quite grim, even on the sugar-coated tour you are likely to get. You will be one of the few adults in your community who has stepped inside this institution. Your conscience and common sense will dictate the next steps.

Talk to public officials. Most likely a commission or other type of public body oversees the juvenile detention facilities in your community. Chances are that an outsider rarely attends the meetings. Go to a meeting and share what you saw on your "tour," or what you have seen as a result of volunteering.

Volunteer to help a kid in detention. Overcome your fear. The youth incarcerated in these facilities are really just children, often more pathetic and childish than other children their age. You will be surprised at how easy it may be to develop a relationship with incarcerated kids. One of the most successful volunteer programs in one inner-city juvenile hall is run by the senior citizens from a wealthy outlying suburb, who come in weekly to tutor the kids.

There is no more rewarding experience than helping a youngster most of society has turned its back on. You can volunteer to teach an art class, coach sports, or provide career counseling. *Anything* you offer in these facilities will make a big difference.

Girls get locked up too. In one city, a coalition of women's organizations recognized that the girls in their detention facility were particularly neglected. They put out a call for volunteer mentors, and within days dozens of women (lawyers, teachers, office workers, artists) eagerly volunteered. All it took was letting women know that the girls needed their help.

Demand humane treatment for kids in jail. Most of the time, our so-called juvenile justice systems operate without any public scrutiny. Youth in trouble become the outcasts of the community. People are both angry and afraid of them. You can play a critical role in bringing about a more humane and sympathetic approach.

Parents Against Abuse of Children. A concerned parent in Sacramento, California, alarmed by the abuse she saw in the juvenile hall, formed this organization. Their media blitz resulted in a grand jury investigation and an FBI probe.

Support rehabilitation, not punishment. The evidence is in. Locking up children does not help. Study after study documents that rehabilitative programs work much better than large, institutional locked facilities. Special schools, residential treatment, daily counseling, and job-training programs make a positive difference in the lives of troubled youth. Here are some ways you can support these programs:

- **Contact the media** when they portray teenagers in a negative light, or subtly imply that kids of a particular race are all criminals or drug dealers. Racial prejudice leads to policies aimed at revenge rather than help.
- **Vote against more prisons for kids.** Use the prison debate to talk about the importance of prevention, the high cost of detention, and developing alternatives to locking kids up.

- **Write your police chief** and say that you want police in your community to talk to parents or send kids to community agencies rather than arrest so many youngsters. Protest if you hear about a youngster who has been treated unfairly by police. Suggest that the police run a diversion program that places youth in therapeutic community programs instead of lockup.
- **Oppose legislation that increases punishment for kids.** Enough already. We punish more kids than any other country in the world. It's not working. But most of the legislators in America think that they are going to win votes if they introduce one more bill increasing sentences of youngsters.
- **Keep kids out of adult jails.** It is illegal to put children in jail with adults, but it is a common occurrence. While in jail, kids are often abused by older inmates. The suicide rates of children in adult jails is a national disgrace. Call your local sheriff's department to find out if kids are kept with adult prisoners. Tell them that you will report the illegality if it's not corrected.

- **Find out about judges and then vote accordingly.** The juvenile court judge determines what will happen to most kids who get arrested. Find out who the judges are in your community. What is their record on kids? What is their position on alternatives to incarceration? Sooner or later, you will get a chance to campaign and vote for or against them.

It is easier to build strong children than to repair broken men.

—Frederick Douglass

Resources

Organizations

Center for the Study of Youth Policy
University of Michigan
1015 E. Huron
Ann Arbor, MI 48104-1689
(313) 747–2556
This group has many publications on juvenile justice issues.

Center on Juvenile and Criminal
    Justice
1622 Folsom Street, 2nd Floor
San Francisco, CA 94103
(415) 621–5661
Contact them to learn about alternatives to detention and how to advocate in your community.

National Council on Crime and
    Delinquency
685 Market Street, Suite 620
San Francisco, CA 94105
(415) 896–6223
Ask about their research and publications on crime prevention and delinquency.

Youth Law Center
114 Sansome Street, #950
San Francisco, CA 94104
(415) 543–3379
This national organization files lawsuits against correctional systems that are abusive to youth.

Chapter 26

Befriend a Homeless Family

It's boring being homeless. You don't have no food. When we were panhandling, the rich people would say, "You're not homeless," and they wouldn't give us any money. Once we had to live out of a car for five months, all of us, four kids and my father. We weren't in school then. It's cramped and smelly and boring in your car when you have to sleep in it. You have cops showing up at your car saying you can't sleep here. It's really dirty. We had to go to the lake to take a bath.

—Edward, age eight

Know the Facts

We all grew up believing that only in third world countries did children have to beg in the streets. Not any more. The number of homeless families and children is burgeoning. Estimates range from 100,000 to 500,000 homeless children on the streets *every night.*

- More than one-third of the homeless are families, the fastest-growing component of the homeless population.
- Lack of resources for families means that homeless families are the people most likely to be denied shelter.
- The median income of families headed by young adults has declined in the past 15 years more than incomes declined during the Depression.

Life in a homeless shelter is crowded, noisy, restrictive, and sometimes dangerous. At most shelters, families can stay only a limited number of nights before moving on to some place else. Often shelters are closed during the day, and mothers are left to wander the streets with young children.

School is not a haven for homeless youngsters. Many homeless children do not attend school, or they change schools frequently. Other children are often cruel to a child when they hear he or she is homeless. Teachers are sometimes insensitive to their situation in requests for children to bring in money for parties or field trips.

The life of a homeless child is dangerous, fragmented, and without any sense of security.

What You Can Do for Homeless Kids . . .

. . . At Home

Be tolerant.   If you are angry that a mother is panhandling with her three children, keep in mind that your anger is better directed toward the government.

Share your food with a homeless family.   If you are walking home from a restaurant with leftovers, leave the food on a bench, or give it to someone. You can also dash into a store and buy baby food or other staples and give them in lieu of money. Many fast-food outlets have gift certificates you can keep in your pocket to pass out to hungry people.

One woman who walked by homeless people every day on her way to work made a routine of waking 20 minutes early to make a half-dozen peanut butter sandwiches to give away. Relatives and friends started giving her family-sized jars of peanut butter to help.

Become informed.   Learn about homeless issues from a homeless advocacy group in your area. To find a group, contact the National Alliance to End Homelessness (see Resources).

. . . In Your Community

Volunteer in a shelter for homeless children and families.
Homeless children's lives are so typically undernourished that they can benefit from the simplest things. Once a week you could help children bake cookies or learn to make lasagna. Or you could organize a softball team, plan a barbecue, or organize a trip to the movies. Or you could just be a good listener.

> This was the funnest day of my life!
>
> —Five-year-old homeless boy, after seeing the ocean for the first time on an outing organized by a volunteer

Here are some tips:

- **Don't make these children into "homeless kids."** These kids had a life before they became homeless. See them as individuals, not as part of some sociocultural group.
- **Don't expect a cuddly kid.** Don't just gravitate toward the cute, young children. The angry teenager who doesn't say thank you when you bring her a birthday present needs consistent attention too.
- **Don't expect an immediate return on your investment.** Sometimes the kindness you have shown, and its rewards, will not blossom for years. You cannot always say, "I helped this family and now they are better."

Adopt a family.   Help a newly housed family set up an apartment. A week's supply of basic groceries, household appliances, your old set of dishes, a refrigerator in the garage, can help a family back to self-sufficiency. Things to start up a house are always important. Call a homeless agency to make contact with a family.

Donate material goods to a homeless program. Call the program to find out what is most needed. There is always a big demand

for anything having to do with pregnancy or the care of infants. One mother had to keep her newborn in a milk crate because she had no crib or bassinet. Always donate clean, mended clothes.

> I try to make it as homey as I can for my kids in the shelter. I try to make it as best as I can wherever we're at so it's not as hard on them . . . We had our own room in one shelter and I had my daughter all set up in one area with her own little bed. On the other side of the room we had my son in his little area. Amy had her own little Disney sheets and pillow-cases and stuffed animals. My son had all his artwork, his drawings, all his little personal things . . . Every night as I watch my kids go to sleep I want to cry.
>
> —Homeless mother

Help build affordable housing. If you believe that decent housing is a basic human right, you are not alone. Today, many organizations are working to expand affordable housing. Through volunteer labor and donations, Habitat for Humanity International builds and rehabilitates homes at an average cost of $35,000. Find out how you can help (see Resources).

Support Youth Build, USA. This project provides high school dropouts with vital work skills while they build and rehabilitate housing for the homeless and the poor. Adequate federal funding would allow communities throughout the country to establish this valuable program (see Resources).

Join the Public Debate: Work for the Solution— Affordable Housing

Public housing is the only way many poor people can stay off the streets. Homelessness escalated dramatically when the federal government suddenly withdrew 70% of its support for public housing in the early 1980s. Support the expansion of federal funding for public housing.

Locally, you can lobby your planning or redevelopment commission to promote affordable housing initiatives in your community, and the targeting of federal housing funds to the truly needy. You could even volunteer to be on the commission that oversees housing policy. Join with others in fighting for affordable housing. Contact the Council of Community Housing Organizations for information (see Resources).

Remember: Homelessness is caused by lack of jobs and lack of affordable housing.

Resources

Organizations

Council of Community Housing
   Organizations
409 Clayton Street
San Francisco, CA 94117
(415) 863-6566
Send for information on developing low-income housing in your community.

Habitat for Humanity International
121 Habitat Street
Americus, GA 31709-3498
(912) 924-6935, ext. 304
Contact them to order information about programs, bumper-stickers, and brochures.

National Low Income Housing
   Coalition
1012 14th Street, N.W. #1200
Washington, D.C. 20005
(202) 662-1530
Ask this advocacy organization about publications and alerts; it can refer you to local and state organizations.

National Alliance to End
   Homelessness
1518 K Street, N.W., Suite 206
Washington, D.C. 20005
(202) 638-1526
Ask about information and advocacy on the homeless; send for publications and newsletters.

Youth Build USA
366 Marsh Street
Belmont, MA 02178
(617) 489-3400
Contact them to initiate or support a youth program that builds low-income housing.

Chapter 27

Promote a Children's Bill of Rights

Never doubt that a small group of thoughtful,
committed citizens can change the world.
Indeed it is the only thing that ever has.

—Margaret Mead

Know the Facts

"The Little Engine That Could" story that opens this book is true. In 1991 a handful of committed citizens in San Francisco, led by Coleman Advocates for Children & Youth, worked to amend the city charter to guarantee a minimum level of funding for children. The charter amendment set aside a portion of the property tax for child care, health care, job training, libraries, and recreation programs for children.

The campaign for the Children's Amendment was a political experiment to see if the growing number of polls documenting public concern about children would translate into support for funding—even if it meant sacrificing other needs. *The experiment worked*—even in the city with the lowest percentage of children in the country. It was a powerful statement about our collective stake in children.

Every community in America has the potential to make putting children first an official policy. Every community will do it differently: an amendment to a charter or local constitution, a petition drive, a local ordinance, a decree from the mayor, a referendum, or a letter-writing campaign. It may articulate general principles or actually create a new funding source.

What You Can Do
for Children's Rights

Understand the lessons of "The Little Engine That Could."

- Going directly to the people can be more effective than going to the traditional political establishment.
- People who care about children must take the initiative, and not wait for politicians to do it for them.
- An election is an ideal forum in which to make the case for children. It provides lots of opportunities to educate the public.
- Voting for something they believe in empowers people and motivates them.
- Children are a winning issue. There is no real argument against investing in children. Once the issue is made public, no one will publicly debate against it!
- Children's rights are everyone's issue. You'll find many surprising allies in a community-wide public debate.
- Winning a victory for children means that politicians will pay more attention to children's needs.

Moral blackmail of the political establishment? Yes! The San Francisco press reported that local politicians secretly opposed the Children's Amendment, but were scared to make their opposition public. It seemed that only when children's fate was decided behind closed doors could politicians oppose putting children first. A public election turned the usual political lip-service into support for concrete change.

Learn what you need to know.

- Is your community aware of the problems of its children? Has information been gathered that documents the unmet needs of children? Are there interested individuals or groups with the capacity to mount a public education campaign?
- Are children's needs underfunded in your community? Is your political establishment likely to make children a higher priority without a legal mandate?
- Are there political, civic, or community groups that could form a coalition to spearhead a children's initiative?

- How have child-related ballot measures such as school bonds fared in your community?
- Is there a potential funding source for an election campaign?
- Will powerful groups oppose a children's initiative? How can these groups be successfully opposed?

What will work in your community? Think about the possibliities. You could initiate a ballot measure, charter amendment, ordinance, or legislative resolution that would:

- set aside a portion of the property tax (or other revenue source) for children's services, as was done in San Francisco;
- prevent budget cuts in children's services;
- create a special taxing district for children's services;
- establish a new fee specifically earmarked for children's services;
- articulate your community's philosophy, goals, or guaranteed rights for its children;
- require your community to develop an annual plan for its children; or
- require a children's impact statement for all relevant legislation (much like an environmental impact statement).

"Cut the bull, pass the bill!"

Steps for mounting a children's campaign.　Find an organization to take the lead. Don't go it alone. Approach a child advocacy group, the children's hospital, the Junior League, the League of Women Voters, the PTA, unions, churches and synagogues, or a coalition of children's service providers to spearhead a campaign for children. Then take these steps:

- **Document the need.** Gather data about the unmet needs of children, the amount of money spent, and the amount it would cost to provide additional services.
- **Develop an organizational structure to mount a campaign.** Form a new coalition, set up a steering committee, or organize a campaign committee.
- **Draft a proposal.** Get the help of lawyers and policy experts.
- **Petition the voters.** Mount a formal petition drive to place something on the ballot, or an informal drive to put pressure on the community leaders.
- **Enlist widespread support.** Get prominent people to endorse the children's campaign—well-known community leaders, representatives from every neighborhood, community organizations, political clubs, religious organizations. Don't forget to enlist groups that are not traditionally associated with children, such as unions, environmentalists, and child-oriented businesses (such as children's clothing and toy stores).
- **Develop community education materials.** These include brochures, public service announcements, signs, and bumperstickers.
- **Get editorial support and media coverage** from local newspapers, radio, and TV stations.

Mounting a community-wide campaign for children is not easy. It could take several years to plan and execute. If it entails a vote by the electorate, it could even lose. But no matter what the outcome is, if it mobilizes concerned citizens and educates the public, children win.

> Cautious, careful people, always casting about to preserve their reputation and social standing, never can bring about reform.
>
> —Susan B. Anthony

Resources

Organizations

Coleman Advocates for
    Children & Youth
2601 Mission Street, #804
San Francisco, CA 94110
(415) 641-4362
Write or call for an information kit
that will help you get started in your
community.

Chapter 28

Reach Out to a Child in Foster Care

Foster care is unique in that natural parents hate the system for "taking" their child. The foster child hates the caseworker for leaving him in a strange home. . . . The foster parents wind up hating the system that has promised to back them up with services for this child, and then finds excuses for never being there when they are needed. Foster care has become, not a solution to our family problems, but one of the biggest causes of family breakdown.

> —Foster parent, quoted in the report of a national commission on foster care

Know the Facts

Nothing is more painful to a child than the feeling of not belonging anywhere. But this is what often happens to children who are removed from their families and placed in the custody of the state. For too many children, our overburdened child welfare and foster-care systems are failing.

A 1978 national commission report on foster care in the United States began, "With some admirable exceptions, the foster care system in America is an unconscionable failure, harming large numbers of children it purports to serve." Not much has changed since then. In fact:

- **The number of children in the child welfare system has risen dramatically** in the past five years, to over 400,000. Many of them have been abused, neglected, or abandoned; many were born addicted to drugs used by their parents; and many suffer serious psychological or physical problems.
- **But as the need for foster care increases, the number of available foster parents in the United States has dropped**—from an estimated 137,000 in the mid-1980s to 100,000 today.

- **The human and financial resources of the foster-care system are grossly inadequate.** In many states the cost of boarding a large dog in a kennel is higher than the rate paid to foster parents to raise a needy child. And 65% of foster parents have incomes below the national average.
- **Foster children are often the victims of double neglect**—first by their parents, then by the public agencies that are supposed to be caring for them. Our prisons and welfare rolls are filled with "graduates" of the foster-care system.

What You Can Do for a Foster Child . . .

. . . At Home

Provide respite for a foster parent. Foster parents are often under a great deal of stress—caring, with limited resources, for children who are disabled, or whose behavior is very provocative, or who need constant physical care. Like any parent—and often more so!—they need a break. Find out if your county has a formal "respite program" for which you could volunteer; or contact your local foster-parent association or welfare department to offer help.

Become a foster parent. You can be a foster parent in more than one way. Open your home on an emergency, short-term basis to children who need immediate shelter; or make a commitment to raise a child for several years—or until the child is 18. Many communities now have "fost-adopt" programs as well, in which parents agree not only to raise a child, but to adopt the child if the birth parents' rights are terminated.

Every county has a foster-care recruitment and licensing agency. Call your local welfare department foster-care unit and find out about regularly scheduled orientation sessions. Ultimately, you take a brief training program and your home is licensed. The process can take months, and includes more red tape than many people care for—but the rewards of being a foster parent can change your life, to say nothing of the life of a child. If *one* American family in 500 became a foster family, there would be no shortage of homes for the thousands of abused and neglected children with no place to go.

Consider adoption. All children should have permanent homes. Children whose parents are unwilling or unable to care for them need an adoptive home. Ideas about adoption have changed dramatically in the past 20 years. Social agencies used to think that only healthy, Caucasian infants had a real chance for adoption. Now children are being adopted at all ages, and with all kinds of disabilities; and children of all races are being placed in racially matched homes.

People considering adoption should be stable and sensitive, in good health, and able to give a child love, understanding, and patience. Most adoption agencies recognize that many different kinds of people can be loving, effective parents (this includes single parents). If you are thinking about adoption, consider adopting a "hard-to-place" child who badly needs a home.

. . . In Your Community

Donate money or needed items to a fund for foster children. Because public funding for foster care is so low and children's needs are so great, many communities have started private fund raising to pay for such things as Christmas presents, music lessons, orthodontia, school supplies, and summer camp. Ask the welfare department in your community whether such a fund exists. If it does not, consider starting one.

Two ideas that work: One church in Connecticut started an Adopt-a-Social Worker Ministry. Volunteers from the congregation donate their money, services, and goods to the children on the caseload of a given social worker. In another city the local newspaper conducts an annual fund-raising campaign for children in foster care.

There are 1,500 foster-parent associations in the United States. The one in your community will be pleased to help you find a way to donate needed funds and services for children in foster care.

Become a citizen advocate for a foster child. Many communities now have an organized program of Court Appointed Special Advocates (CASAs), who serve as the community's eyes and ears on behalf of foster children. The CASA program was begun in 1977 as a way to ensure that abused and neglected children don't face more abuse and neglect by the system. CASAs are trained volunteers, appointed by a juvenile or family court judge to be an independent "voice" for a child in court.

According to the National CASA Association, a CASA volunteer has three main responsibilities: "to serve as a fact-finder for the judge by thoroughly researching the background of each assigned case; to speak for the child in the courtroom, representing the child's best interests; and to continue to act as a watchdog for the child during the life of the case, ensuring that it is brought to a swift and appropriate conclusion." Over 28,000 CASA volunteers serve in 520 programs in all 50 states. The average caseload is light—one or two children. Volunteers are ordinary citizens; no special or legal background is required. To find the CASA program nearest you, contact the National CASA Association (see Resources).

What one CASA volunteer did. One CASA volunteer, asked to intervene in a family with three neglected young children, was able to save an endangered family: First, she helped place the children with a relative. Then she arranged for the mother to take special parenting classes. She also arranged for the oldest child, who was marginally retarded, to get special education that he had been deprived of before. Over time, she monitored the mother's progress in counseling and in the classes. Eventually, she recommended that the children be returned home to the mother.

Write a letter protesting cuts in the foster-care budget. Foster care is already woefully underfunded. Many foster parents spend a great deal of their own money on a child's necessities because their monthly payments don't even cover food and clothing. The foster-care budget provides no money for child care. Cutbacks at welfare departments mean that fewer social workers are handling mounting caseloads, and that children are being neglected. Children are easy to set aside at budget time because they don't have a voice in the system, but you do. Don't be silent.

Join the Public Debate: Support Public Policies and Programs that Help Families Stay Together

Most experts in the field now agree that much more effort should go into keeping children with their birth families whenever possible. A public bureaucracy, no matter how well intentioned, is not a good parent; and an underfunded bureaucracy is often abusive.

Although no child should be kept in danger, demonstration projects have shown that it is sometimes much better, and much cheaper, to offer families the support services they need to raise their children—such as drug counseling, parenting assistance, respite care, and job training—than it is to support children in the foster-care system. The National CASA Association notes that "the annual foster-care bill to the taxpayers is over $6 billion, but the cost in human potential is even greater."

Remember: All of us deserve a home in this world. Do your part to help a forgotten child find one.

Resources

Organizations

National CASA Association
2722 Eastlake Avenue, E, Suite 220
Seattle, WA 98102
(206) 328-8588
Ask how you can find the CASA
program in your community.

National Foster Parents Association
226 Kitts Drive
Houston, TX 77024
(713) 467-1850
Contact them to learn more about
foster parenting, or to begin a foster
parent organization.

Adoption
National Adoption Center
1500 Walnut Street, #701
Philadelphia, PA 19102
(215) 735-9988
(800) TO-ADOPT
Their slogan is, "There are no
unwanted children . . . just unfound
parents." This group promotes
adoption opportunities, with the
focus on kids with special needs; they
have a computerized adoption
exchange, fact sheets, and brochures.

National Adoption Information
   Clearinghouse
11426 Rockville Pike, Suite 410
Rockville, MD 20852
(301) 231-6512
Send for information brochures and
packets; ask about referrals.

Chapter 29

Empower Kids to Save the Earth

I don't want the earth to die before I do.

—Greg, age 13

Know the Facts

The degradation of the environment presents the ultimate crisis for our children: It threatens the very air they breathe, the water they drink, and the earth they walk on. From ozone depletion to global warming, from rainforest destruction to species reduction—these problems appear every bit as threatening to the new generation as the threat of nuclear war was to their parents.

In homes, schools, community centers—any place where youth gather—kids are listening and taking heroic actions to save the Earth. In this pivotal decade, we can empower kids to make a difference to our threatened planet.

What You Can Do . . .

. . . To Help Children Understand the Environment

Be a good example.   If you follow environmentally sound practices, you will help children make the connection between simple action and consequences for the entire planet. You'll find dozens of guides that can help you with precycling, recycling, composting, energy efficiency, and environmentally safe products.

Join an environmental organization.   Share the information you get with children. "Think globally, act locally" is a powerful message for children.

Collect a children's environmental library. Put the library in your home, or donate it to your school or neighborhood library. The Sierra Club and the book *Earth Child* offer lists of environmental books to get you started and your librarian can help you select appropriate titles. Send for free materials, then donate them (see Resources for more ideas).

. . . To Help Children Make Friends with Living Things

Plant a tree and care for it. Plant a tree in your yard, or in a community planting organized with neighbors. Bring nature to the hard concrete of the city to help clean the air, provide habitat for animals, and be a visible connection to the natural environment.

Help children plant a garden. Adopt an ugly patch of ground in your neighborhood, clear it of rubbish, and start a garden. Plant wildflowers in a vacant lot or along a road.

Turn your backyard into a wildlife habitat. The National Wildlife Federation has a backyard wildlife program to help you design and designate your own yard as a wildlife habitat.

Don't let children abuse animals. A recent report by the American Humane Society notes that "a child who learns aggression against living creatures is more likely to exhibit aggressive behavior against people as an adult." Do not ignore even minor acts of cruelty. Intervene if you see a child being cruel to animals, and express your concerns to parents. Margaret Mead warned, "One of the most dangerous things that can happen to a child is to kill or torture an animal and get away with it."

Help kids experience natural environments. Most kids living in the inner city never leave the neighborhood. Take city kids outdoors—on hikes, picnics, and bird-watching trips—so they can experience natural environments, plants, and animals. Local, state, and national parks may have special programs for children, as does the Sierra Club. Children can also have fun participating with you in an antilitter campaign or a beach clean-up day.

Many children, perhaps because they are small and closer to the ground than we, notice and delight in the small and inconspicuous. With this beginning, it is easy to share with them the beauties we usually miss because we look too hastily, seeing the whole, not its parts.

—Rachael Carson, *A Sense of Wonder*

. . . To Help a Child Become an Environmental Activist

Help a child write a letter or join a demonstration. Environmental activism is a wonderful way to teach democratic values. Even small children can express their opinions about the environment. They can draw pictures of what they want their neighborhood to look like; they have ideas about saving forests and protecting dolphins. You can send their letters to local city planners or national policy makers. Children can also participate in local demonstrations—something they feel proud of and remember the rest of their lives.

Kids for Saving Earth. Kids for Saving Earth, the largest children's environmental group in the world, has teamed with Target Stores and Hanes to produce a program for elementary schools or clubs called "Target Earth, Study and Reward Program for Schools." This program is packed in a nifty "suitcase" and offers a complete educational/activist curriculum combining home projects with group activities. It includes special resources for rainforest projects, backyard habitats, and organizing an Earth Expo for your school or community. Kids get certificates for completion of environmental activities, which they can present for free T-shirts, decals, and treats at local Target stores. Classes or clubs can earn an award plaque. It's a complete environmental program—and the best part is, it's free!

Help a child get involved in the children's environmental movement. "Children manage to find the most creative and compelling ways to focus the attention of their parents and other adults on the importance of protecting our environment," says Vice President Al Gore. "Our children are the hope for the environment and the caretakers for our future." Groups like the Toxic

Avengers of El Puente, the Green Guerrillas, SAVE (Students Against the Violation of the Earth), and YES (Youth for Environmental Sanity) have started recycling programs at their schools, planted trees in their community and adopted trees in faraway rainforests, and even sued their school boards over toxic chemicals in milk cartons.

Bring a children's perspective to adult community planning. KidsPlace in Seattle, Washington, began a program that puts kids on city commissions and brings a much-needed perspective to planning. One ten-year-old member of the Water Commission was asked what he thought of a model for a waterfront project presented by an architect. He replied, "I don't like it—there's no place to touch the water." The project went back to the drawing boards.

. . . To Teach Kids About Toxics

Kids are more vulnerable to toxics than anyone else. Pound for pound, children's bodies take in more food, water, and air than adults. A growing child whose brain and bone marrow are still developing, or who is at the crawling and "taste testing" stage, is at greatest risk.

Take sensible precautions at home. If you arm yourself with the facts, you will be able to better protect children in your own home. Here are some things you might do:

- Avoid hazardous art supplies. Always look at the labels to make sure products are nontoxic.
- Find household cleaning supplies that are less toxic and less environmentally dangerous, such as various mixtures of baking soda, salt, vinegar, lemon juice, and borax.
- Dispose of toxics carefully. Follow EPA guidelines.
- Move your young video game addict at least two feet away from the screen, and consider appliances with lower radiation levels.

Get the lead out! Public health officials say lead is the leading environmental threat to children, whether they live in public housing or neat suburban homes—74% of all private housing built before 1980 contains some lead paint. One in nine children under age six has enough lead in his or her blood to be at risk. Children with high lead levels are six times more likely to have reading disabilities. Here's what you can do:

- Have your child tested for lead poisoning at an early age, as a regular part of well-baby care.
- Have your water or house tested for lead if you fear it could be a problem. Use safe methods when you renovate.
- Wet sweep your house regularly—lead paint dust is a common source of poisoning.

Monitor schools and other child-serving facilities. We'd like to think our kids are safe at school, but it's not always so. In San Diego, California, a group called School Pesticide Use Reduction was formed in response to the discovery that harsh pesticides were often used excessively without concern for child safety in school buildings and grounds.

Let us remember in our deliberations, the effect our decisions may have on the next seven generations.

—Invocation of the
Iroquois Tribal Council

Resources

Kids' Organizations

Kids for Saving the Earth
P.O. Box 47247
Plymouth, MN 55447-0247
(612) 525–0002
Ask for information about "Target Earth, Study and Reward Program for Schools."

YES (Youth For Environmental Sanity)
706 Frederick Street
Santa Cruz, CA 95062
(408) 459–9344
Order their *Student Action Guide* ($3.95).

Other Organizations

Consumer Information Center
P.O. Box 100
Pueblo, CO 81009
(719) 948–3334
Send for brochures on environmental safety.

Environmental Hazards Management Institute
10 Newmarket Road
P.O. Box 932
Durham, NH 03824
(603) 868–1496
Order the "Household Hazardous Waste Wheel," which lists safer alternatives and ways to dispose of toxic home wastes.

National Center for Environmental
Health Strategies
1100 Rural Avenue
Voorhees, NJ 08043
(609) 429–5358
Send for a free information package.

National Wildlife Federation
Correspondence Division
1400 16th Street, N.W.
Washington, D.C. 20036-2266
(202) 797–6800 (for list of
publications)
(800) 432–6564 (for merchandise)
Send for information on backyard
wildlife habitats.

Switchboards

EPA Hot Line
(800) 424–9346

Publications

*Earth Child: Games, Stories,
Activities, Experiments and Ideas*,
by Kathryn Sheehan and Mary
Waidner, Ph.D. Tulsa, OK: Council
Oak Books, 1991. Each chapter has
a wonderful bibliography and
resource section pointing out
organizations, books, and other
resources for children and adults.
To order, call (800) 247–8850
($16.95, plus shipping).

*50 Simple Things Kids Can Do to Save
the Earth*, by the Earth Works
Group. Kansas City: Andrews &
McMeel, 1990. To order, call (800)
826–4216 (also available in libraries
and bookstores).

*50 Simple Things You Can Do to Save
the Earth* and *Kid Heroes of the
Environment*, by the Earth Works
Group. 1400 Shattuck Avenue #25,
Berkeley, CA 94709. To order, call
(510) 652–8533 (also available in
bookstores).

*Green Guide, An Educator's Guide to
Free and Inexpensive Environmental
Materials*, edited by Pat Suiter. San
Francisco: Sierra Club, 1991. To
order, write the Sierra Club, 730
Polk Street, San Francisco, CA
94109, or call (415) 776–2211
($8.00 plus shipping). They also
have a free *Sourcebook* that lists all
educational materials, including a
suggested reading list.

Seventh Generation. Mail-order
catalog for alternative products and
books. Write to Seventh
Generation, Colchester, VT 05446-
1672, or call (800) 456–1177.

Chapter 30

Support Real Family Values

Explain family values to 15 million kids in poverty.

—Bumper-sticker produced by Coleman
Advocates for Children & Youth

Know the Facts

Politicians are adept at offering lip service to "family values." But when it comes to offering parents the kind of help they really need to raise their children in America today, rhetoric is not enough.

Being a parent is a difficult job to begin with, and many parents do not earn enough to support their families. Some lack jobs or shelter; others confront days when there's nothing to eat in the fridge, the TV's busted, or there's no money to call a doctor.

Some single parents feel lonely and isolated because they have no one with whom to share parenting responsibilities. Most parents feel guilty: They are trying valiantly to shield their children from the conditions we as a society have created. They wonder why it feels as if they are struggling upstream alone—why it is so hard to raise children, and why their children are not as well off as they were.

Child-savers need to be parent-savers too. Parent-bashing is in. The discussion of "family values" is a subtle form of it. The attack on welfare moms is more overt. If the answer is to blame "bad parents," then we're all off the hook. We don't have to address poor education, unemployment, lack of housing. Don't get sucked into the parent-blaming game. Parents, as well as children, have problems when they don't have support and opportunity.

Remember: Every time you help a parent, you are helping a child.

What You Can Do to
Promote *Real* Family Values

"Adopt" a single parent or adolescent mother. The only way we can end the isolation of single parents is to reach out. You can offer the parent respite from constant child care, transportation to appointments, outings, special treats on holidays, or other practical assistance. Contact your social services department or one of the organizations listed in Resources to find a program.

Assist a family in crisis. Share the wisdom you have gained as a parent. Unless someone helps at the beginning of the crisis, the situation often gets worse and children end up having to be removed from their home. This is not only a disaster for the child, but it costs all of us a fortune to have that child raised by the state. Almost every social service department in the country has family preservation (child protective service) units to keep families in crisis together. You can help in such an emergency with food, transportation, babysitting, or even temporarily taking a child into your home.

Volunteer at a parental stress hot line. Call United Way or the Child Abuse Hot Line (see Resources) to find out if your community has this valuable resource, which provides support to harassed parents whose children may be at risk of abuse. Hot lines are generally run on the steam of compassionate sensible volunteers. One hot-line volunteer told this story:

> An anxious mother called our hot line saying that her two year old was driving her crazy—"No, no, no"—all the time, and she was ready to swat him. I told her that this was fairly typical behavior for a two year old, and suggested some ways for avoiding battles (if Jimmy refuses to eat, just take the food away without making a fuss about it). I think the real problem was that the experience of being a mother did not meet her expectations, and she had no one to talk to about this. I linked her up with a mother's group, and told her I would call her next week to see how things were going.
>
> When I called back, she sounded better. She had contacted the mother's group and had been able to relax and laugh a little at some of Jimmy's antics. She thanked me for listening to her and making her feel like she was not a terrible mother. I told her that I

had raised kids and knew exactly what she was going through. In fact, it made me feel good to be able to help someone out in the same situation I had been in.

Donate books on parenting. Increasingly, school libraries are developing a special section for books on parenting skills. Parents are invited to the school to take advantage of the parenting collection. Ask your librarian about creating such a section if it doesn't exist.

Teach a "get-acquainted" class. These classes are for immigrant parents with limited English skills who are unfamiliar with American customs. Because of the language barrier, these parents often depend on their children to do adult tasks like calling the doctor. When you give a parent new skills, all of the family benefits. Contact newcomer organizations in your community to explore this possibility.

> We had a family from the church who watched over us. They took me to school on my first day and helped us find a place to live, and found my mother a job. My mother said they were our American angels.
>
> —Ninth-grade Vietnamese girl

Give a mom a break. Have your church or synagogue sponsor a "mother's morning off" program, where parents can bring children for a few hours of special activities and have a break. Never underestimate the family value of reducing stress on mothers!

When you reach out to a parent:

Don't say, "Let me know if I can do anything for you."

Do say, "I have a few free hours this weekend. I'd be happy to come over and stay with your children while you go shopping or take in a movie."

Join the Public Debate:
Support Parent Action

Eminent pediatrician T. Berry Brazelton says, "The parents of this generation are beginning to feel empowered. They are asking hard questions, demanding answers, and they are ready to fight for what they need, for their children and themselves." Dr. Brazelton wants parents to use their potential political powers—after all, they're raising the next generation!

In response, he and others have started this country's first political action group for parents: Parent Action. It is the only national organization for *all* parents, and is intended to serve parents in a way similar to how the American Association of Retired Persons (AARP) serves seniors.

Parent Action is currently working to increase respect for the role of parenting. It advocates policies that support parents, such as parental leave; secures discounts on services and goods; and publishes a quarterly newsletter and periodic action alerts. More important, it connects parents with a nationwide movement for families. Parent Action is one of our children's best hopes of having their voices heard on a national level. Join—even if you're not a parent.

Remember: We must demand from our government what we demand from every family—the recognition that our most precious resource is our children.

Resources

Organizations

Family Resource Coalition
200 South Michigan Avenue, Suite
   1520
Chicago, IL 60604
(312) 341–0900
Send for information on programs
near you that support parents.

National Parent Aide Association
332 South Michigan Avenue, Suite
   1600
Chicago, IL 60604
(312) 663–3520
This group can help you find the
parent program nearest you.

Parent Action (see Multi-Issue
   Resources)
This is the leading parent advocacy
organization in the United States.

Switchboards

National Child Abuse Hot Line
1 (800) 4–ACHILD
Call to find a parental stress hot line
near you—either to volunteer, or to
get help for yourself or others.

Chapter 31

Make Your Vote Count for Kids

Never before has there been a constituency so popular, but with so little political clout.

—Connecticut Senator Christopher Dodd

Know the Facts

Politicians kiss babies on the campaign trail, but after the election it's usually a different story. Why?

- Children don't vote.
- Children don't make political contributions.
- Children don't hire lobbyists.

No politician in America believes that his or her political future rests on what he or she does for kids. **Together we can prove politicians wrong.** A close local race will often be decided by less than ten votes per precinct! In recent elections a shift of only 10,000 votes per contest would have changed the outcome in many Senate races.

Who's for Kids and Who's Just Kidding? With this slogan the Coalition for America's Children launched a campaign in 1991 to give a political voice to children. The concept is simple: Figure out who's for kids and who's just kidding, and then vote for the pro-child candidate. "The days of kiss the baby for the camera, and run after the election, are over," declared Bob Keeshan, aka Captain Kangaroo, during the 1992 presidential campaign.

What You Can Do to Make Your Vote Count

FIGURE OUT WHO'S FOR KIDS

Apply this test to every candidate.

Unless otherwise indicated, 1 = no, and 2 = yes.

1. Does the candidate have a solid pro-child platform?
   (1 point for support of each issue)
   - comprehensive health care for all children
   - tax policies that benefit low- and middle-income families raising children
   - educational excellence and financial support for public schools
   - expansion of publicly funded affordable child care and quality preschool education
   - adequate income supports, job training, and housing for the poorest families
   - regulation of industries that exploit children, such as tobacco, alcohol, and commercial TV
   - adequate funding for rehabilitation, counseling, and other services for children in need

2. Are the candidate's positions on children highlighted in his or her literature and advertisements? (1 or 2)

3. Does the candidate have a written position statement on children? (*Note:* Position statements are a routine part of every campaign. Call the campaign office to have the children's statement sent to you. If there is no position statement, that should tell you everything you need to know. Just calling a campaign to ask gives the candidate the message that children are important.) (1 or 2)

4. Does the candidate have any experience, or track record in supporting children's causes? (*Note:* If candidates are incumbents, check their track record. If they have been in Congress, the Children's Defense Fund will have rated their votes; you can order CDF's annual nonpartisan congressional voting record. Inquire about the candidates' track records from the League of Women Voters, the child advocacy organization in your state, the PTA, or another group you trust. The staff of these organizations in

your state capital can tell you how cooperative candidates have been on children's issues. If the candidates are not incumbents, check their background. Have they been active in the PTA? on the board of a children's organization? in a school bond campaign?) (1 or 2)

5. Does the candidate have an innovative and *specific* plan to implement any of the policy positions in question 1? (This one's extra credit. If yes, add 2 points per plan.)

6. Does the candidate use code words or stereotypes that appeal to prejudices against poor people, welfare recipients, racial minority youth, single parents, sexual minorities, immigrants, or any other part of the American family? (If yes, cross them off your list now.)

Now tally each candidate's score. Vote for the candidate with the highest score. Let all candidates know why you have made your choice.

Remember: When it comes to support for children, rhetoric means nothing. Pictures of children on slick brochures mean nothing. Specific commitments to take action for families with children mean everything.

Attend a candidates' forum and ask about children. During campaigns, candidates running for office are out every night speaking to community groups. Attend and ask questions. Call campaign offices to find out about a meeting near your home.

One question can make a difference: One politician came back from an afternoon of door-to-door canvassing and told his staff that there was a lot of concern in the community about child care. *One voter* had asked him his position on child care. One voter!

Register pro-child voters. Only 55% of eligible voters actually voted in the 1992 election, and this turnout was considered great progress in that it reversed a 20-year downward trend. Children, sometimes called "orphans of the ballot box," lose when their supporters don't vote, particularly because the number of households with children continues to decline. Unfortunately, lower-income younger voters tend to be the ones who aren't voting, and they are the ones who are most likely raising kids. What's more, a growing number of our youngsters have parents who are not citizens and therefore can't vote. Our kids need every pro-child voter they can get!

- **Register to vote yourself.**
- **Take voter registration forms to child-care centers.** You'll find voter registration cards at the post office, the public library, and the Registrar of Voters in your community. Keep a stack of them, and deliver them to local day-care centers, PTA meetings, recreation centers, and other places where parents are likely to be.
  Get schools to encourage voting. Get your local high school to register all eligible seniors. The League of Women Voters can help with this type of project.

Work for a strong pro-child candidate. Here are some ways you could help out during an election:

- **Be a campaign volunteer.** This may entail phoning, staffing an office, walking a precinct, getting out the vote on election day. *All* campaigns desperately need volunteers.

- **Write a letter** to the editor of your local newspaper expressing your strong support for the candidate. This is some of the best publicity a candidate can get. It's free, it reflects community support, and it's better than a lot of slick brochures.
- **Send a postcard to ten friends** telling them why you support this candidate, and urge them to vote for the candidate.
- **Donate** to the campaign of your candidate if you can.

Help sponsor a candidates' forum on children.   Urge an organization in your community—a church or synagogue, labor union, civic organization, neighborhood association, or parents group—to sponsor a candidate's forum on children's issues. Candidates go to several forums a day—on different issues and with different constituencies. The first candidate's forum on children in one U.S. city turned out to be the best attended forum in the entire mayor's campaign, and had a great impact on the winner's policy agenda. Some groups have held forums where the questions are asked by youth themselves. The forum should be well publicized. This is a perfect way to demonstrate to the candidates the importance of children's issues, and to *hold them accountable for their positions and promises.*

> I'm for kids and I vote.
>
> —Bumper-sticker from Coleman Advocates
> for Children & Youth

Resources

Organizations

Coalition for America's Children
1710 Rhode Island Avenue, N.W., 4th
    Floor
Washington, D.C. 20036
(202) 857–7829
Ask for information on how to do a candidates' forum, report cards, canvassing, and materials for a VoteKids drive.

Children's Defense Fund (see
    Multi-Issue Resources)
Ask for their nonpartisan congressional voting record.

Coleman Advocates for Children &
    Youth
2601 Mission Street, #804
San Francisco, CA 94110
(415) 641–4362
Call to order the "Kids Vote" bumper-sticker.

League of Women Voters
1730 M Street, N.W., Suite 1000
Washington, D.C. 20036
(800) 435–5551
Send for posters, videotapes, booklets, and brochures on voter registration.

National Association of Child
    Advocates (see Multi-Issue
    Resources)
Ask for help finding advocacy groups that issue report cards.

Project Vote
1424 16th Street, N.W., Suite 101
Washington, D.C. 20036
(202) 328–1500
This group can help you get involved with voter registration drives throughout the United States.

Publications

You Can Change America, by The
    Earth Works Group. Berkeley, CA:
    Earth Works Press, Inc., 1992. This
    is a good, easy-to-read handbook on
    political involvement.

Part 2

REVIEWING THE BASICS:

SKILLS YOU NEED TO MAKE EVERY KID COUNT

Give Time:
How to Be
an Effective Volunteer

Volunteers are the lifeblood of many organizations that help children. There are as many ways to volunteer as there are individuals—because each one of us has special skills, talents, and passions that can serve as the basis for a rewarding volunteer experience.

Step One:
Decide What Type
of Work You Want to Do

As you've seen from this book, "volunteering" isn't limited to working with an individual child or a group of children. It can also mean identifying a children's agency that needs some help in the office—answering phones, getting out mailings, organizing a fund raiser, greeting the public. Before you plunge in, get as clear as you can about who you would like to work with, what you would like to do, and how many hours a week (or a month) you would like to do it.

If You Want to Work Directly with Children . . .

. . . *What are your talents?* Even if you don't have traditionally "marketable" skills, anything that you can share is a way you can help. Cooking, storytelling, knitting, fishing, bowling— if you love doing it, you'll communicate your enthusiasm. The more experiences children have, the more chances there will be for something to spark an interest that might change a life!

. . . *Who do you picture yourself with?* Do you see yourself cuddling a three-year-old on your lap? Maybe you see yourself reading to a sick child in a hospital. You might want to spend time with adolescents who are starting to get into trouble and need to be rescued—the "tough cases," kids who are already involved with gangs or drugs. Perhaps you see yourself sharing your wisdom as a parent with other parents under stress.

. . . *How much energy do you have?* Do you see yourself coaching a kids' team? Would you like to do art activities with just one or two children? How about taking a group of teens to a museum? Or playing your guitar for a small audience?

. . . *Where would you like to work?* Make it easy on yourself—volunteer in the setting that suits your needs and abilities. Consider the possibilities:

- outdoor recreation and parks programs, on local playgrounds and in city parks
- homeless shelters
- programs serving immigrant and refugee children
- the local library
- a children's hospital
- after-school tutoring programs

- community centers
- elementary school classrooms
- day-care centers
- telephone hot lines

When you work directly with children, you are often free to propose a particular activity or create a program. Many organizations serving children would welcome an afternoon art class, or a sports program, or a field trip to a museum, or a reading circle—whatever your creative contributions might be. And the overworked staff will certainly appreciate your energy and enthusiasm!

If You Want to Work Behind the Scenes . . .

. . . *What sort of help are you willing to provide?*   Being a volunteer doesn't mean you have to suffer! Think about the things you enjoy—or at least wouldn't mind—doing. Don't prepare to offer your typing skills when typing drives you up the wall.

Children's organizations typically need help with a wide range of activities, from the menial to the professional:

- answering phones
- entering data into a computer
- getting out a bulk mailing
- researching an issue
- helping with bookkeeping, taxes, or financial reports
- writing grant proposals
- identifying potential donors in the community; soliciting funds
- planning an event to raise money or awareness about an issue
- writing or designing annual reports and public relations materials
- providing legal advice
- serving on a board of directors

Don't downplay the importance of helping out in the office. If you have just a few hours a week, and you don't want to get *too* involved but you want to do "something," helping around the office can be an extremely valuable offering for a busy children's agency.

Remember: When you help a children's organization—in any of the above ways—you will actually be helping large numbers of children.

Step Two:
Finding a Place to Volunteer

Many communities have volunteer centers—there are more than 400 across the United States. To locate the volunteer center in your community or get other types of help in making a good match, call the Points of Light Foundation (see Resources). You can also call your local school district, churches or synagogues, or community centers. Be resourceful—there are many different ways to locate children's organizations that might need your help.

Here are some factors to consider when choosing a site:

- Does the organization provide volunteer training?
- Does the organization clearly state its expectations for volunteers?
- Does the organization supply you with the materials you need?
- Will you get help and supervision when things get tough?
- Do you feel welcome there?

Step Three:
Getting the "Job"

Many people don't realize that landing a good volunteer experience takes work and usually a number of false starts. Children's organizations are, by and large, understaffed and overburdened nonprofits. Most of them can use a volunteer, but may not have a staff person formally designated to help integrate a volunteer into their work. So how do you make sure that your offer of to help does not become a hindrance to an agency? Here's some things you can do to avoid frustration:

- **Send the agency a short letter** describing your skills and interests, and follow it up with a phone call. This will make it easier for them to evaluate how you might fit into an agency's activities.
- **Ask if you can come visit the organization** and have a *brief* meeting with a staff person. This is the best way for both you and the agency to judge how well your contribution will mesh with their needs.

- **Be clear about your availability and your limits.** Make sure the organization knows how long you think you'd like to volunteer. The goal is to make a consistent, reliable contribution—whether it's two hours per week or two hours per month.
- **Try to set up a trial period** of several weeks or several months. After that time you can have a better sense of what you're getting out of the experience, and the organization can determine if their needs have changed.

What Do Children Need from Volunteers?

Children need respect.   A woman who volunteers to work with homeless children offers these ideas, which you can apply to all children:

1. **Get down on your knees with children.** Make eye contact, and treat them like individuals with different life stories, problems, and needs. Think before you speak. Some of the questions you probably should *not* ask a homeless child include: "How did you get to be homeless?" and, "Was it fun living in your car?" You even have to be leery about "Do you like school?" because many children who are between schools may be embarrassed about not attending regularly.
2. When working with homeless or otherwise disadvantaged children, **applaud the child when he or she succeeds in even the smallest way.** Find out what the child is interested in. Does he like art? Does she want to learn how to play softball? Understand that these children are at their lowest in terms of feeling good about themselves and many are suffering from neglect, abuse and deprivation. By finding a way to make them feel like they are special, that they do something really well, you can give them control over some aspect of their lives.
3. **Working with children can be very easy.** Go to a library, pick up a few books, take a child on your lap, and pretty soon you will have

two, or three, or four surrounding you. Don't worry about "age appropriateness," as many of the older children are soothed just by listening to a story. Just sitting quietly, listening, and sharing an experience with a group is positive.

Children need opportunity.   Many young people never get the simple opportunity to leave their own neighborhood and see how other people live. How can young people grow up with a sense of a future if they are limited by the horizon immediately surrounding them—a horizon that may include drugs, crime and a graffiti-spattered environment? How can young people imagine themselves going to college when they've never set foot on the local college campus? It's hard to picture yourself doing more than slinging burgers if no one has ever showed you what the inside of an office is like, how people treat each other there, how they dress.

If you are a volunteer tutor, remember that you are also a model and a resource. Whether you are tutoring teenagers in math, helping with homework, or doing an art project together, try to incorporate broader horizons in your work: Offer to help her write a resume. Let him accompany you to your job one day. Loan her a good book. Take him on a tour of an art museum. In just an hour, you can open up a world of possibilities.

Resources

Points of Light Foundation
   (see Multi-Issue Resources)
Ask how you can contact
organizations that need volunteers.

United Black Fund, Inc.
1012 14th Street, N.W., Suite 300
Washington, D.C. 20005
(202) 783–9300
They can help you contact
organizations that meet needs of
African-American children.

Volunteer for Kids
(800) 950–3453
Sponsored by the Child Welfare
League of America, this group is
linked with 450 children's agencies
that need volunteers.

Give Resources:
How to Be
an Effective Donor

Government budgets have faced drastic cutbacks, and we are losing many services that we have taken for granted. Desperate appeals for funding fill our mailboxes. Even services such as public education, which we have considered a basic right, have increasingly appealed to the private sector. As concerned citizens, most of us naturally want to do our share.

Donating Money to Children's Organizations

Learn about the Organization

It's best to give to organizations whose work you know firsthand. If you plan to make a significant donation, pay a visit if at all possible.

Take the time to evaluate, and use your common sense. Don't allow yourself to be rushed into making an unwise donation. For instance, make sure you agree with both the ends and the means. Recreation for disadvantaged children is a commendable goal, but find out how many children will actually go to camp.

If you want to take a deeper look:

- Ask for references from other reputable organizations in your community.
- Request a "statement of functional expenses" so that you can compare program claims in brochures with actual line item expenses. If the organization spends only a small amount on the program that interests you, you may want to choose another organization. As a rule of thumb, no more than 30% of the funds should go to-

ward fund-raising expenses (many organizations spend much less), and a minimum of 60% should go directly to programs.

- If a charity receives more than $25,000 a year, you can get a copy of the federally required annual Form 990 filing from the organization.

Feel comfortable asking about what concerns you. For more ways to learn about an organization, see Resources.

Be Wary of Solicitors

Be cautious with door-to-door or phone solicitations from organizations you don't know. Check the name—is it really the charity you think it is? Ask the solicitor if he or she is a volunteer, an employee of the organization, or an outside paid fund raiser on a commission. If you are asked to contribute to a fund-raising event, ask how much of the ticket cost counts as a contribution. How much of your donation do you want to go toward expenses rather than direct services?

Remember: Don't be intimidated. If you are asked to give money, you have the right and the responsibility to ask questions on all matters that concern you.

When Your Resources Are Limited

- **Consider making fewer donations of a larger amount.** The administrative costs of thanking donors, processing donations in a computer database, and depositing your check can eat away at your contribution.
- **Subscribe to the organization's newsletter.** Spend some of your time following their advocacy suggestions. Then pass the publications on to friends or colleagues. (You'll save nonprofits a lot of money by telling them if you receive duplicate mailings, or if you prefer not to receive mailings.)

Don't Forget about Planned Giving

A planned gift—a donation in your will—can be a win-win situation. It can have tax advantages for you, and provide continued support of organizations that are important to you. All planned gifts, from a simple bequest to a more complex trust, need to be written into a will. Your attorney, broker, CPA, or insurance planner should be involved in the process. Remember, you can update your will as circumstances change.

Think about how you want your money spent. You may want to be specific—for instance, to support the education of the child of a low-income single parent.

Donating Goods
to Children and Families

One of the most gratifying ways you can help children is by donating everything from food, to office equipment, to art supplies. Throughout this book, we have made suggestions. Here are some guidelines:

- **Find out what they really need.** Try to put yourself into the situation of the receiver. For example, a homeless family may not be able to use costume jewelry, but a craft or theater class might. Before you donate your items, call the organization to find out how you can best provide them with donated goods. Remember that storage can be a problem. Overburdened social service programs may not have the staff or a vehicle to pick up an item— your donations are even more valuable if you can offer to deliver.
- **Avoid gifts that promote stereotypes, violence, or passivity.**
- **Don't overlook any possibilities.** That collection of art materials and scraps, long-abandoned musical instruments in the attic, leftover party food, or even ripening fruit on your backyard tree may be a useful donation to the right organization.
- **Try to make a sustaining commitment rather than a one-time gift.** You can maintain a distinct portion of a program over time by providing lunches for children on outings, or supplies for an ongoing craft program.

One grandmother collects used items to help homeless families set up housekeeping when they are able to find permanent homes. She collects sets of dishes, appliances, and so on from neighbors and a widening community who have heard of her good works. She stores and distributes materials from her garage—friends with trucks help deliver her housewarming kits.

What About Tax Deductions?

You may have noticed this notation when you have made a donation: "Tax deductible to the extent of the law." You must itemize deductible donations to charity of money or property on the long form 1040 in order to qualify for deductions. Depending on your personal tax situation, donations may be tax deductible to varying degrees. "We

are tax-exempt" does not necessarily mean that contributions are tax-deductible. Principal among tax deductible groups are 501(c)(3)'s, commonly known as non-profit organizations. Charitable organizations that are tax deductible include churches, schools, libraries, parks, and recreation.

Keep receipts for goods and your canceled checks for monetary donations. Although the value of your volunteer time is not deductible, out-of-pocket expenses (including transportation costs) are allowed. If you give to an event or receive a promotional gift, only the amount that exceeds the fair market value can be deducted. You may want to keep a special file to document your charitable activities. If you have further questions, you can call the IRS information number (see Resources) to be connected to your regional office.

Resources

Council of Better Business Bureau's Philanthropic Advisory Service
Dept. 024
Washington, D.C. 20042-0024
Send for the brochure *Tips for charitable giving.*

The Foundation Center
79 5th Avenue
New York, NY 10003-3076
(800) 424–9836
This is a national organization with regional centers; send for information on foundation fund raising; order publications or get references.

Internal Revenue Service
(800) 829–1040
Ask for Publication 561, *Determining the Value of Donated Property,* and Publication 562, *Charitable Contributions.*

National Charities Information Bureau (NCIB)
Dept. 259
19 Union Square West, 6th Floor
New York, NY 10003-3395
(212) 929–6300
Ask for their guide, which evaluates national charities based on philanthropic standards.

Give 'Em Hell: How to Be an Effective Child Advocate

Charity makes you feel good about what you do.
Justice makes everyone feel good about what is being done.

—Kenneth Tieman

Are you outraged . . .

- . . . when politicians say they love kids and then vote against everything children need, like prenatal care and funding for schools?
- . . . when schoolchildren have to sell candy door-to-door to keep the school library open, while there is plenty of money for prisons and highways?
- . . . when rich tobacco companies can get away with using cartoons to seduce our children into smoking—an addiction that can kill them?

Tap that outrage! The outrage you feel is the very thing that will enable you to make the world a better place for children. People will try to tell you that there is something wrong or unhealthy about being angry— "Mellow out," "Be good to yourself," "Don't make waves," "Don't alienate anyone." They are wrong. The trick is to focus your anger, to make change happen. You can use that outrage—or anger, or concern—to become an advocate for children.

Throughout this book we have asked you to contact the White House, to write a letter to the editor, to meet with your legislator, to testify at your school board, or to get your neighbors to sign a petition. You may have noticed that even when there are laws to protect children, there is usually no agency that takes the initiative to see that they are obeyed. Laws related to children's television programming, child labor, child abuse, beer advertising, and equal access for children with disabilities *all* require citizens, like yourself, to fight to have them implemented. Chances are, you have never done anything like this before—but you can. If you take the time now to master some easy principles and techniques, you can begin to change the world for children.

Remember: Pick a fight that is big enough to matter, but small enough to win.

Telephone Calls
Are Quick, Easy, and Effective

Find the numbers. Sit down right now and post near your phone a list of the ten numbers you may want to call over the next year: mayor, city council, school board, superintendent of schools, state legislators, U.S. representatives and senators (they will have local offices), White House, TV stations, and local newspaper. You can use the list at the end of this book to get you started. **Don't be embarrassed if you don't know who half of these people are. Very few people do. Consult your phone book, local library, League of Women Voters, Registrar of Voters, or local newspaper.**

Get the nerve. "Hello, please give the message to the mayor that I strongly object to the city closing the children's library on Saturday

afternoon." It's over in less than 60 seconds! Most likely, you will not have to answer questions, debate anyone, or even talk to anyone other than a receptionist. But at the end of the day, when the mayor's staff tallies the calls, your message will have an impact.

You can ask to have the official return your call, but don't be upset if a staff person calls you back instead. Often it is more effective to talk to the person working directly on the issue.

Become a regular caller. Once you discover just how easy it is to call key sources of power, you will do it frequently. It can be part of your routine before going off to work—a healthy way to deal with pent-up frustration after reading the paper.

The Power of the Written Word

Taking the time to put your opinions in writing is in itself a statement about the depth of your concern. Furthermore, it creates a tangible document that can be circulated, that will be kept in the file for a long time, and which they must respond to.

Remember: It is more important to write *any* letter—two sentences—than to not write at all. At the very least, your position will be noted. You need not type. You need not make elaborate arguments. You can even send a postcard—buy a stack from the post office to keep ready for when your righteous anger compels you to act.

Use your letter more than once. If you take the time to articulate your position to a legislator, you might want to send a similar (or the same) letter to your local newspaper.

Or you could **turn your letter into a petition** and have a dozen of your friends sign it. In one city, a group of neighbors started a handwritten petition drive to keep libraries open. Soon people were writing and circulating their own petition. And sure enough—the libraries were kept open.

Another citizen advocate started a **mini-movement on a street corner.** A critical vote on a children's playground was coming up at the city council. He typed the phone numbers of council members, and handed out his home-grown fact sheet. Pretty soon he had recruited six sympathetic passers-by, who joined him in distributing fliers.

One particularly energetic advocate regularly writes up her own position on issues when she goes to a meeting. She circulates copies, and much to her amazement has found that her ideas sometimes find their way into official reports!

Use the copy machine.   The best way to hold public officials accountable is to send copies of letters to other key people. (Photocopying machines and computers make this easy!) A letter to the mayor about poor conditions in a city-run day-care center could be sent to the media, other politicians (maybe even the mayor's political adversaries), parents at the center, and the city administrator running the center. Each one knows the others have gotten the letter. No one can claim ignorance of the problem. *Your chances of getting action skyrocket!*

Speak Out!

Most people have almost a phobic fear of speaking in public. For the sake of our children, try to overcome this. You may not realize it, but dozens of meetings occur every month in your community where important decisions are made and where your views could be heard.

Find the forum.   Call city hall, your board of education, your elected representatives, or various city departments to find out about hearings and community meetings on the issues of interest to you. Sometimes community newspapers have a calendar. Don't be surprised if you are one of only a few people attending these meetings— all the more important that you be there. Also, don't necessarily wait until your issue is on the official agenda—that may never happen. Either ask to have it placed on the agenda, or find out if there is open time for public testimony on "new business."

MAKING A GOOD SPEECH

It is often not the experienced speaker who commands attention from public officials, but rather the average citizen who is nervously speaking for the first time. (In fact, being nervous often helps— people know you are sincere and they empathize.) If you are not a city government regular, are not on the payroll of a group that will

benefit from your proposal, but simply a concerned voter and tax-payer—you *will* get attention.

Here are some hints about speech-making:

- **Keep it short, short, short.** Public officials have short attention spans, and important points take little time to make. For example, a uniformed police officer gave a one-sentence speech: He said that he wanted the city to do something for children while they were young, so he didn't have to arrest them when they got older. Period. That was it, and that was all that was needed.
- **Use a personal example.** Focus your speech on things you know about personally—problems of children you know (your own included); evidence you have witnessed or gathered (the homeless children sleeping on the doorstep of your business); the concern of a group you belong to (your neighborhood club, women's group, professional association).
- **Use your passion.** Too many people try too hard to disguise their feelings, thinking this makes them appear more objective. Showing the depth of your concern actually makes you a more credible and compelling speaker.

Meetings: Face to Face
with Decision-Makers

Meeting face to face—with your elected officials, your newspaper editor, or the heads of various city agencies—can make a big difference in the impact your ideas have. Here are some points to remember:

- **Get in the door.** Getting a meeting with "important" officials can take persistence and work—putting requests in writing, calling back many times, tolerating schedule changes. Stick with it.
- **Get their attention.** Busy public officials are often distracted and give you very little time. State your position quickly and with as much drama as possible. You could even practice a snappy one-minute opener that succinctly summarizes your position.
- **Don't go alone.** Sometimes people in power will try to intimidate you, or conveniently "forget" what transpired at a meeting. You need support, assistance, and a witness. It can be helpful (although not necessary) to be accompanied by someone who is known in the community.
- **Have the specifics.** Document your concern. Bring with you a specific suggestion for a remedy—in written form, if possible, so that the official can use it later.

"I guess the climate has changed. Could you explain that children's bill to me again?"

- **Don't forget to follow up.** Agree to some specific method—another meeting, a written response, a phone call, referral to another person.
- **Write a thank-you letter.** The real reason for this goes beyond courtesy. It reiterates commitments made, and lets the person know you will not accept empty promises.

Using the Media: You Can Make the Difference

Child advocates must learn to use the power of the press. In one city, when the press began to report that the local health department was about to cut the only free children's dental services, all of a sudden the services were back in the budget. All the lobbying, calling, protesting, reports, and testifying didn't accomplish one-tenth of what one newspaper story accomplished. Here are some things you can do to influence the media.

Plant a children's story.   Journalists are always looking for stories. Keep track of which TV, radio, or newspaper reporters cover stories related to children. They will welcome your specific leads or creative ideas—a child who overcame great odds, a family treated unfairly by the city bureaucracy, a program that is being cut. After a few contacts, you may be surprised to find reporters calling you for your "expert" opinion!

Complain about distorted or unfair coverage.   **Never believe anything just because it is in the paper or on TV.** Facts are often distorted, or just plain wrong. When you learn to listen for what is *not* being said, you'll begin to notice things—for example, that the "experts" being quoted are always the same ones, that the costs of the welfare system are never compared to the costs of the prison system, or that stories on inner-city youth are always about violence and never about positive aspects of these youngsters' lives.

WHAT MEDIA WATCHDOGS SHOULD LOOK FOR

- How frequently does the media run stories on children's issues? Are the stories given good placement, or are they stuck in the back or at the end of the newscast with items about cooking or cats in trees?
- Is the coverage entirely accurate? Is it slanted with innuendo, or missing key facts, or taken out of context, or overly sensationalized? Is it editorial comment disguised as news?
- Does the story include varied and balanced sources? Does it include the views of parents and kids themselves?
- Does the coverage address root causes of the problem, or does it merely focus on disturbing symptoms?
- Does the story include proposed solutions? Solutions generated by all sides of the debate?
- Does the story portray children sympathetically (both in pictures and descriptions)? Most kids are earnest, energetic, and resourceful. Many are extraordinarily articulate. Would you know that from the media coverage?

Make yourself known.   If you read a story that you like, call or write the author of the story, the news editor, or the editor. If you read a story that you don't like, do the same. The same goes for TV news. Journalists are more concerned about public opinion than they let on. If you are particularly incensed, you could mobilize an organization or several well-known people to request a meeting with the editorial board.

Write a guest editorial or letter to the editor.   Take note of the types of letters and guest editorials your paper prints. This will help you present your ideas in the way most likely to be published. You can send a letter or editorial to more than one paper. Especially at election time, letters can mean much-needed publicity for your cause. (Don't give up on getting published. Sometimes it takes many submissions. But it's worth the effort—thousands of people will read it.)

Insider Secrets

Be   dramatic!   When you have the time and energy, try an attention-grabbing strategy. Public officials are more likely to take note, and the media may even cover it. Think about the parents who sent the mayor poignant letters from their children when their day-care center was about to close, or the mother who brought her child in a wheelchair to a hearing and asked city council members to look after her because she had no place for the child to go after school.

Use an "official-sounding" name.   Even if you have only three friends on your side, give yourselves a name like "Neighbors for Better Playgrounds." Make simple stationery (using a computer and a copy machine) with your official name. Suddenly, you're a force to be reckoned with.

Don't become known as a kook.   Every community has a few people who are nuisances to public officials and finally get the door slammed in their face. Avoid the following:

- **Never cry wolf.** No politician wants to spend time (or even worse, make public statements) about something that proves not to be a problem. Don't rely on gossip—check the facts.

- **Don't have unrealistic expectations.** Give public officials adequate time to make corrections. Bring them problems over which they have authority (for example, don't ask local officials to curtail defense spending.) Remember, they must work within existing laws and governmental structures.

Propose solutions whenever possible.   Most people expect public officials to figure out the solutions to problems. That's okay, but not nearly as good as proposing a workable solution yourself. Instead of saying, "I have five kids and no one will rent to me. What are you going to do about it?" say, "I think we should amend the city's rent ordinance to outlaw discrimination against families with children." If you have a solution, you are ten times more likely to get action: Keep the lights on in the playground for two more hours, or outlaw alcohol advertising on city buses.

Democracy is infectious. Involve other people. Talk it up with family and friends. Once you have learned to speak out, you will never be silent again.

Resources

Publications

Childhood's Future, by Richard Louv. Boston: Houghton Mifflin, 1991. This is a passionate call to make children a priority.

Fairness Is a Kid's Game: Children, Public Policy, and Child Advocacy in the States, by David Richart and Stephen Bing. Louisville: Kentucky Youth Advocates, 1987. This is a handbook about what makes advocacy effective. To order, call (502) 895–8167.

The Kids' Guide to Social Action, by Barbara A. Lewis. Minneapolis: Free Spirit Publishing, 1991. To order, call (800) 735–7323.

So You Want to Make a Difference: A Key to Advocacy, by Nancy Amidei. Washington, D.C.: OMB Watch, 1991. This is a great primer on becoming an advocate. To order, write OMB Watch, 1731 Connecticut Avenue, N.W., 4th Floor, Washington, D.C. 20009-1146, or call (202) 234–8494.

Sources

The information in this book came from a number of sources, many of which are listed at the end of each chapter. Some of the material comes from newspaper (*New York Times, Washington Post, San Francisco Chronicle*) and journal articles. Most of the material comes from reports and studies by academic institutions, governmental agencies, and private research organizations, most notably:

American Academy of Pediatrics, Elk Grove Village, IL
American Medical Association, Chicago, IL
American Public Welfare Association, Washington, D.C.
Brown University Child Study Center, Providence, RI
Bureau of Labor Statistics, Washington, D.C.
Carnegie Corporation of New York, New York, NY
Center for Community Change, Washington, D.C.
Center for the Future of Children, Packard Foundation, Palo Alto, CA
Center for Population Options, Washington, D.C.
Center for the Study of Social Policy, Kids Count Project,
    Washington, D.C.
Center on Budget and Policy Priorities, Washington, D.C.
Center on Rural Elderly, Kansas City, MO
Centers for Disease Control, Atlanta, GA
Charles Stuart Mott Foundation, Flint, MI
Child Protection Reports, Silver Springs, MD
Child Welfare League of America, Washington, D.C.
Children's Defense Fund, Washington, D.C.
Children's Safety Network, Washington, D.C.
Committee for Economic Development, New York, NY
Congressional Budget Office, Washington, D.C.
Food Research Action Center, Washington, D.C.
Hudson Institute, Indianapolis, IN

National Center for Children in Poverty, Columbia University, New York, NY

National Center on Education and Economy, Rochester, NY

National Child Labor Committee, New York, NY

National Coalition on Homelessness, Washington, D.C.

National Commission on Children, Washington, D.C.

National Commission on the Role of the School and the Community in Improving Adolescent Health, American Medical Association and National Association of State Boards of Education, Alexandria, VA

National Committee for Prevention of Child Abuse, Chicago, IL

National Commission to Prevent Infant Mortality, Washington, D.C.

National Network of Runaway and Youth Services, Washington, D.C.

National PTA, Chicago, IL

Project Vote, Washington, D.C.

Select Committee on Children and Youth, U.S. House of Representatives, Washington, D.C.

Sierra Club, San Francisco, CA

Stanford University and the National Bureau of Economic Research, Stanford, CA

U.C.S.F. Medical School, San Francisco, CA

United Nations Children's Fund, New York, NY

U.S. Census Bureau, Washington, D.C.

U.S. Department of Transportation, Washington, D.C.

U.S. National Institute of Justice, Washington, D.C.

U.S. Surgeon General, Washington, D.C.

William T. Grant Foundation Commission on Work, Family and Citizenship, Washington, D.C.

Multi-Issue Resources

Center on Budget and Policy Priorities
777 North Capitol Street, N.E., Suite 705
Washington, D.C. 20002
(202) 408–1080

This national research and policy think-tank analyzes and publishes reports on children's issues.

Children's Defense Fund
25 E Street, N.W.
Washington, D.C. 20001
(202) 628–8787
(202) 662–3678 (Information Hot Line—tape recording)

CDF is America's leading child advocacy organization. They have information on all children's issues; newsletters, publications, action alerts to help you become a successful advocate; posters and other materials you can share with friends and colleagues.

Child Welfare League of America
440 First Street, N.W., Suite 310
Washington, D.C. 20001-2085
(202) 636–2952
(800) 8-KIDS-80 (The Kids Campaign)

This national membership organization for children's service providers has action alerts, newsletters, and information on issues and services.

Coleman Advocates for Children & Youth
2601 Mission Street, #804
San Francisco, CA 94110
(415) 641–4362

Call about videos, bumper-stickers, information concerning this book, and information on starting local child advocacy organizations and initiatives.

National Association of Child Advocates
1625 K Street, N.W., Suite 510
Washington, D.C. 20006
(202) 828–6950

This is a membership organization for child advocacy groups. Call to find an organization in your state or community.

National Association for the Education of Young Children
1509 16th Street, N.W.
Washington, D.C. 20036
(800) 424–2460

This group has extensive educational resources on child care, child-hood development.

National Black Child Development Institute
1023 15th Street, N.W., Suite 600
Washington, D.C. 20005
(202) 387–1281

Ask about health, welfare, education, and child-care issues. Call or write for information packet and contact with local affiliate.

National Crime Prevention Council
1700 K Street, N.W., 2nd Floor
Washington, D.C. 20006-3817
(202) 466–6272

Contact them for information on public education resources and training on crime prevention, drugs, alcohol, community involvement, youth participation.

National League of Cities
1301 Pennsylvania Avenue, N.W., Suite 600
Washington, D.C. 20004
(202) 626–3000

Their "Children in Cities" project identifies and shares information on children's projects in cities throughout the country. They can help you find key organizations in your city. Ask for their booklet on making government work for your city's children.

National PTA
700 North Rush Street
Chicago, IL 60611-2571
(312) 787–0977

A wealth of information on everything from how a busy parent can get involved in education to helping children develop self-esteem to school choice; ask about journals, newsletter.

Parent Action
2 North Charles Street, #960
Baltimore, MD 21201
(410) PARENTS

Parent Action advocates policies that support parenting, and promotes a nationwide movement for families.

Points of Light Foundation
(800) 879–5400

This 24-hour information line is a major clearinghouse for information on volunteer opportunities and services in your community; 400 affiliates nationwide.

United States Committee for UNICEF
333 E. 38th Street, 6th Floor
New York, NY 10016
(212) 686–5522

Send for information on the state of the world's children.

Appendix 2

Handy Phone Numbers

Let Your Voice Be Heard on the Political Level

National Policymakers

President

White House opinion line
(202) 456–1111 or
(202) 456–1414 (24 hours)
President of the United States
1600 Pennsylvania Avenue
Washington, D.C. 20500

Congress

United States Senate and House of
    Representatives
Washington, D.C. 20515-0001
(202) 224–3121 (Capitol switchboard)

Senator: _____

Senator: _____

Representative: _____

State Officials

Governor: _____

State senator: _____

State representative: _____

Other: _____

Community Officials

Mayor/County administrator: _____

City council/Board: _____

School Board: _____

Other: _____

_____

_____

Let the Media Know What You Think

National Networks

The following are for general comments. For comments concerning children's programming, see Resources, chapter 1.

ABC
Audience Relations
77 West 66th Street
New York, NY 10023
(212) 456–7477
10 A.M. to 12:30 P.M.; 2 P.M.
to 4 P.M. (weekdays)

CBS
Audience Services
524 West 57th Street
New York, NY 10019
(212) 975–3247
10 A.M. to 11:30 A.M.;
2 P.M. to 3:30 P.M. (weekdays)

NBC
Audience Services
30 Rockefeller Plaza
New York, NY 10112
(212) 664–4444
9 A.M. to 12 P.M.; 2 P.M. to 5 P.M. (weekdays)

PBS
Corporation for Public Broadcasting
P.O. Box 50880
Washington, D.C. 20091-0880
(800) 356–2626 (24-hour public
comment line)

FOX
P.O. Box 900
Beverly Hills, CA 90213
(Include name of show on envelope)
(310) 277–2211

Local TV Stations and Newspapers

_____

_____

_____

_____

_____

_____

We hope this book has stimulated you to come up with your own ideas and innovations, and we'd like to hear about them. Let us know what you've done to make every kid count!
You can write Coleman Advocates for Children & Youth at 2601 Mission Street, #804, San Francisco, CA 94110, or call (415) 641-4362.

About Margaret Brodkin and Coleman Advocates for Children & Youth

Margaret Brodkin, ACSW, LCSW, is Executive Director of Coleman Advocates for Children & Youth in San Francisco. Founded in 1975, Coleman Advocates has emerged as one of the most innovative and influential child advocacy organizations in the country. As a result of Coleman Advocates's efforts, San Francisco became the first American city to guarantee funding for children each year in its city budget.

Author photograph: Beatriz Coll